The
Flying Roll

The Time Shall Come When Man Shall Be Cut Off

WE ARE THE LAST GENERATION

ROBERT DENNIE

Fulton Books
Meadville, PA

Published by Fulton Books 2024

Artwork by Dackery L. Williams

ISBN 979-8-89221-152-9 (paperback)
ISBN 979-8-89221-153-6 (digital)

Printed in the United States of America

TABLE OF CONTENTS

and teachers at schools, murdering people in our synagogues, churches, clubs etc.

16. On page 53, those misleading pastors need to repent. As men and women of GOD, we must commit ourselves to a faithful stand on truth. Decisions should be made with fear and trembling.

17. On page 56, Back to Prophecy

18. On page 59, The coming of Christ is also set forth in the following document.

19. On page 62, The fact is that the saints take the kingdom from those four, which is in fact proof that those are the last kingdom of man.

20. On page 65, Picture G: The time of the kingdom of Christ.

21. On page 66, Picture: The Sealing of the 144,000

22. On page 68, Picture: Today we are living the current events of GOD's Prophecy

23. On page 69, Biblical Word Definitions

24. On page 71, Copy Explaining Prophecy

25. On page72, The prophecy of GOD is proven true by world history

26. On page 74, We are in the last generation.

27. On page 79, GOD has promised to bring great tribulation upon this last generation.

28. On page 86, After the rapture when Jesus takes saints away.

29. On page 88, He shall scatter among them the prey, and spoil, and riches: Yea, and he shall forecast his devices against the strong holds, even for a time (Daniel 11:24)

30. On page 90, Conclusion of Revelation: The Fourth Kingdom

31. On page 95, Teaching Outline

32. On page 103, Contents at a Glance

33. On page 107, Appendix A: My Chapter Checklist

34. On page 116, Picture: Colossus

35. On page 117, Picture: This document illustrates information which set forth the rise of England to world power.

36. On page 118, Picture: Division of Alexander's Empire 303 B.C.

37. On page 119, Picture: The King of Rome

38. On page 120, Picture: History of Anglo-Saxon England

PREFACE

The Reason I Wrote This Book

For as he thinks in his heart, so is he.

—Proverbs 23:7

In my heart, what I think is that Jesus told me to "write this book" to inform man of the problems that are coming and how to avoid destruction.

From the day I had the dream of holding the Sunday school book, that dream and circumstances stayed with me over the years. I looked for the angel to tell me what the Lord wanted me to do. (The angel said, "I will tell you the Lord's will for you.")

> And the Lord said unto the servants, go out into
> the highways and hedges, and compel them to
> come in, that my house may be filled. (Luke 14:23)

I knew I had the answer from the Lord because He gave me the understanding, which was why I was writing this book. Through prayer and study, I was setting forth a clear understanding of what God's prophecy was for this last generation (the revelation generation).

Because it was not only in prophecy but also in "climate change," the coming end to this earth, along with the killing and destroying of war events.

In this book, I have pointed out a way for God's people to avoid the end destruction coming upon the wicked.

In my book, I explain in detail the rise and fall of all world governments, including the coming kingdom of Christ. That explanation starts with the first world government of King Nebuchadnezzar and lists every rising government in proper order until the coming of the kingdom of Christ.

Which helps us understand where we are in God's prophecy today, because when God releases the flying roll, we need to be walking holy.

INTRODUCTION

Hi, my name is Robert Dennie. This is my first book, and I am not striving to be a term writer because my book is about the revelations, which I studied for fifty years. My age is seventy-nine. In studying the process of writing this book, the question asked was, Why do I want to write a book?

I want to win someone to Christ and inform a lost generation that trouble is coming.

This is an extremely lost generation because there is confusion in the minds of men today. Millions of people are becoming members of the cult QAnon.

And when teaching the prophecy to a confused mind, I take extra steps in my teachings—preface, teaching outline, contents briefly, and chapter checklist, supplying instructions.

The book I have chosen to write deals with circumstances, whereas many can be lost. Hence the name of the book, *The Flying Roll*. In these circumstances, the Lord has said that He is going to send forth a curse across the face of the earth. Depending on the circumstances, everyone on the planet can be affected, won, or lost.

In my life, I had received Christ as my personal savior, and my life changed. I was working a job approximately an hour and one-half from town. We rode to our job in a van. Before salvation, I was gambling on the way to work and drinking and gambling on returning home in time.

I bought a small Bible and studied it going to and coming from work. After three years, I was shopping one day and found a book named *The Book of Revelation*, written by Clarence Larkin and published in 1929.

I became interested in studying the revelations. When I was approximately fifty years old, I began drawing biblical sketches, which are now included in the book. Through studying the scriptures, I found Habakkuk 2:2–3.

> And the Lord answered me, and said, write the vision, and make it plain upon tables, that he may run that Readett it. For the vision is yet for an appointed time, but at the end it shall speak, and not lie; though it tarry, wait for it; because it will surely come, it will not tarry.

I BELIEVE THE SCRIPTURE STATEMENTS WERE SPEAKING TO ME, WHICH IS WHY I WROTE THIS BOOK. I've taken time to look and think about the word and the will of God, and I begin thinking, *Is it possible that a little person like me could play a part?*
<u>IN THINKING, LOOKING BACK TO THE FIRST WORLD TIME OF NOAH, AND GODS PLAN IN DEALING WITH MAN. IF I HAD BEEN THERE LOOKING AT THAT HUGE SHIP, WHICH HAD TO BE THE SIZE OF A FRONTIER TOWN.</u> I would never have believed that huge ship in the middle of a forest was going to clear the grown and go anyplace.

> For my though are not your though, neither are your ways my ways, saith the Lord. For as the heavens are higher than the earth, so are my ways higher than your ways, and my thoughts than your thoughts. (Isaiah 55:8–9)

I thought about Joyce Meyer's book, *Battlefield of the Mind*, as I struggled with the thought that I could have a part in the Bible prophecy.

And as I look at the prophecy and world events today, my thoughts are as follows: We should be concerned about where we are in God's prophecy.

The last four-world kingdoms exist.

1. England
2. USA
3. Russia
4. Japan/China

Today, when talking at family events and with friends, we are confronted with dealing with an educated generation that seeks to rationalize everything. This is where Evangelist Joyce Meyer's book, *Battlefield of the Mind*, comes to mind. This is why we are recommending her book as a foundation for understanding any revelation book, including this one.

I am not saying that you can't understand our book of revelations without reading her book, but it would be far easier if you did.

Preliminary Statement

When we come into contact with the minds of men today, we are dealing with people who have taken intelligence in a backward direction. WITH THAT SAID, WE NOW HAVE MILLIONS OF PEOPLE WHO HAVE BECOME PART OF QANON.

In talking to those people, many of them profess to be followers of Christ, but they are in a cult. This is one of the main reasons that we are suggesting *Battlefield of the Mind*. BECAUSE THE DEVIL IS IN CONTROL OF THE QANONS, AND THEIR THOUGHT PATTERNS ARE DIRECTED BY SATAN.

THE FLYING ROLL

THE TIME SHALL COME WHEN MAN SHALL BE CUTOFF:
This book covers Prophecy, History, Climate
Change and Current Events

Zech. 5:1 Then I turned and lifted up mine eyes, and looked, and behold, a FLYING ROLL, 5:2, And he said unto me, what seest thou? And I answered, I see a FLYING ROLL; the length thereof is TWENTY CUBITS, and the breadth thereof TEN CUBITS. 5:3 Then said he unto me, This is the curse that goeth forth over the face of the whole earth: for everyone that STEALETH shall be CUT OFF as on that side according to it and every one that sweareth shall be cut off as on that side according to it. 5:4 I will bring it forth, saith the LORD of Hosts, and it shall ENTER INTO the HOUSE of the THIEF and into the house of him that SWEARETH FALSELY by my name, and it shall remain in the midst of his house and shall CONSUME it with the TIMBER therof, and the STONE thereof.

II Tim. 3:12 Yea, and all that shall live godly in Christ Jesus shall suffer persecution.

Psalms 37:23 The steps of a GOOD MAN are ORDERED by the LORD.

John 14:15 If you LOVE ME keep my COMMANDMENTS.

THE FLYING ROLL

We cannot look at our circumstances down here and think that we are in a struggle with our fellow men. We are in a fight with the devil.

And a look at our enemy, which is **Trumpism/ Satanism**.

Today we are living in a time when men refuse to accept the truth. Call it politics or whatever, they are looking for ways to accept some idea that goes along with what they want things to be or believe.

Now we must consider Trump's sixty million people, who will not consider reality unless it's forced upon them.

For example, one of Trump's **Proud Boys**, part of Trump's enforcement body, Henry Tarrio, the leader of the Proud Boys, received twenty-two years in prison, along with the fact that numerous other members received large prison sentences as well.

I think I want you to remember that I use **red ink** and **other colors** in this book because prophecy is hard to understand. At the same time, we are serving a **God** who knows **everything** and knows that that would be man's attitude today. FOR THE SCRIPTURE DECLARES THAT THERE SHALL BE A GREAT FALLING AWAY.

> Let no man deceive you by any means: for that day shall not come, except there come, a falling away first, and that man of sin be revealed. (2 Thessalonians 3:3)

TRUMP'S FOLLOWERS ARE THAT GREAT FALL-ING AWAY. Yet God sent forth his **prophecy** to today's generation. We are teaching prophecy to a generation that <u>doesn't believe the truth</u>.

Approximately ten or fifteen years ago, scientists started the explanation of climate change, which the world did not want to be bothered with or believe, and the world continued its way of destroying the planet.

Donald Trump is in control of the Republican Party as of March 17, 2021. "12 Republicans vote AGAINST awarding the Congressional Gold Medal to Capitol Police for their heroism on January 6."

That displays the hatred of Congress for this nation, and law enforcement is supporting and protecting it.

Trumpism represents lies and hate. Furthermore, Trump's Republican Party is now claiming that the attack on the Capitol was not a terrorist attack. A LARGE NUMBER OF TRUMP'S SUP-PORTERS ARE **HATERS.**

Furthermore, through Donald Trump's rallies, he relates to his followers that the COVID-19 we are suffering from came from the Chinese. This caused his followers to hate the Chinese, which is why today the Chinese are afraid to walk the streets. They are being insulted, beaten, and killed.

THE CHRISTIAN CHURCH LEADERS ARE GIV-ING CHRISTIAN MEMBERS' MONEY TO DONALD TRUMP, BELIEVING OUR GOD IS TOO DUMB TO UNDERSTAND.

The fact is that you are God's leaders over the body, given to instruct and guide the body toward righteousness, but you have made a deal with the devil.

So Donald Trump helped you block abortions in nations, and while president, Trump told the Christian community, "I did what you asked me to, so why are you complaining now?"

According to the *Washington Post*, "Trumpism is American fascism."

The following are the **right-wing groups**:

1. **QAnon** is a cult defined by a system of religious veneration and devotion directed toward a particular figure or object. The **figure** upon whom this cult is directed is **Donald Trump.** A **cult** is a term that does not refer to religion at all but is applied to a social movement. Those who accept the beliefs and rituals are members of the religious cults. But many outsiders consider the movement and its followers to be a cult. And numerous members have been charged by the Feds with attacking the Capitol.
2. **Proud Boys** is a right-wing group composed of criminals. The leader has publicly stated that he talked to President Trump prior to January 6, and Trump promised to send the boys to Washington on January 6. Numerous members have been charged by the Feds with the attack on the Capitol. Canada has declared the Proud Boys to be a terrorist group. Furthermore, in 2023, the court declared the Proud Boys to be a terrorist group.
3. **Oath Keepers** is another right-wing criminal group, of which numerous members have been charged by the Feds with attacks on the Capitol.
4. **III Percenters** is another right-wing criminal group. Its numerous members have been charged by the Feds with attacking the Capitol.

There are several other groups involved in the attacks on the Capitol. Numerous members of the said groups are involved in different White supremacist movements, such as the ones below.

1. Texas Freedom Force
2. Nazis and White Supremacists
3. Ohio State Regular Militia

The Lord made it clear in His Word.

> Have no fellowship with unfaithful workers of darkness, but rather reprove them. (Ephesians 5:11)

Supporting Trump means having fellowship with him.

Define **reprove.** It implies an often kindle intent to correct a fault. Donald Trump has not made an effort to reprove them, but he invites them to his rallies because they are his followers.

To reiterate, Donald Trump informed his followers to go to the Capitol building on the sixth of January to prevent President Biden's presidential completion.

We have set forth above the criminal element that Trump was sending to the Capitol, and we say criminal element, because federal law enforcement, as well as other law enforcement agencies, are still prosecuting them.

To reiterate **Trumpism's finances** further, Donald Trump shifted campaign donor funds into his heavily indebted private business after his election loss, Forbes reported.

Curses are part of my prophecy. I talked to my sister-in-law, who told me that no one wants to read a book about curses. And as I considered that, I thought about the COVID-19 we are now facing, and my thoughts were, *How many people want to deal with that?* My answer is none.

We are not given a choice down here on what things we should deal with, which is why we are sending this message forth: to win the loss.

THE MIND OF MAN

In my approach to dealing with the mind of man, as I sorted through my efforts, I thought I had better look at Joyce Meyer's book, *Battlefield of the Mind*. And so, as I looked at the book and perceived a thought, she needs to rewrite a book—*Battlefield of the Mind, Last Generation*. Because her book had numerous answers, I would like to use them myself in my revelation book.

The Lord said in His word.

> And have no fellowship with the unfruitful works of darkness, but rather reprove them. (Ephesians 5:11)

The devil is not asleep; he is sending forth a message to control the minds of men!

It was surprising how many people voted for President Trump in this election, which was approximately sixty-two million. On January 25, 2021, a discussion came on TV that day that Trump was thinking of establishing a third party. Keep in mind that in the past, while he was president, he stated that he wanted to be on Mount Rushmore.

Having said that, should Trump establish a third party, he was going to put his face on our flag. It would be the end of our democracy because Trump was setting forth plans to run his family and members of his administration for the Senate around the country. The GOP is divided over support for far-right extremists.

According to the *Washington Post*, "Trumpism is American fascism." It slanders outsiders and blames them for social and economic ills. It warns of global plots by Jews and shadowy elites. **IT**

ACCEPTS THE LIES OF A LEADER AS A DEEPER FORM OF POLITICAL TRUTH. It reveals anger and dehumanization.

Donald Trump recently went on Fox News, herein the later part of March, and made a statement: "They just walked in and walked out…they were hugging and kissing cops."

Now the said fact is a lie, conforming to the statement just made, "It accepts the lies of a leader as a deeper form of political truth." This is a form of **Satanism**. Furthermore, Trump's members are involved.

The article in the *Wall Street Journal* titled "Jan. 6 Rally Founded by Top Trump Donor, Alex Jones, Organizers Say," discussed her involvement in a conspiracy with Donald Trump and his right-wing criminals. The article was authored by Shalini Ramachandran, Alexandra Berzon, and Rebecca Bauhaus.

Another one of Trump's right-wing conspirators, Steve Bannon, said on his podcast (January 5): "All hell is going to break loose tomorrow. Just understand this, all hell is going to break loose tomorrow. It is going to be quick."

In terms of group coordination, the *Washington Post* stated that the group gathered for coordination before the assault. Donovan Crowl and other members of the Oath Keepers were at the US Capitol on January 6. The article "Be Ready to Fight: FBI Probe of U.S. Capitol Riot Finds Evidence Detailing Coordination of an Assault" could be found under the segment National Security.

The said facts confirmed group corporation and coordination. It was not possible to finance transportation for the enormous number of people involved in Trump's rally without coordination with the groups Oath Keepers, Proud Boys, and III Percenters.

The said facts confirmed a **conspiracy**. We were living in a **lying generation**.

The mind is the leader or forerunner of all actions. Roman 8:5 makes it clear: "For those who are according to the flesh and are controlled by its unholy desires set their minds on a pursue those things which gratify the flesh, but those who are according to the Spirit set their minds on and seek those things which gratify [Holy] Spirit."

This is the reason *Battlefield of the Mind* is necessary in teaching and understanding the revelations and this last generation.

God created this world and us, and in His creation, He gave us the *book of Revelation*, telling us the things that would happen in the last generation.

In creating this world and us, God decided that the last part of this world would be revelations. I didn't know that man could become that intelligent to the point of ignoring God's will about revelations and moving on with his life.

Through this interpretation of prophecy, we sit forth the first-world kingdom and lead you step-by-step to the last four kingdoms of man.

As we look at the Christian community's support for President Donald Trump, they say he is a good president and taking care of this country.

During the debate, President Trump was asked about the right-wing group Proud Boys. He asked them to stand down and stay around. In his speech, he was inviting them to attack the Capitol, calling them forth.

And it is our position: the revelation of events will occur in this world within the next thirty years.

> And I brought him to thy disciples, and they could not cure him. Then Jesus answered and said, "O faithless and perverse generation, how long shall I be with you? How long shall I suffer you? Bring him hither to me." And Jesus rebuked the devil; and he departed out of him: and the child was cured from that very hour. Then came the disciples to Jesus apart, and said, why could not we cast him out? And Jesus said unto them, "Because of your unbelief." (Matthew 17:16–20)

REMEMBER THAT UNBELIEF LEADS TO DIS-OBEDIENCE. As I began to write this book, it became evident to me that I am not equipped to write a book, and for worsening circumstances, it is a book on prophecy. Explaining a book on prophecy is always a greater handful. This is a world full of intelligent people who, for the most part, do not like God's explanations that are not in a 1-2-3 or A-B-C order. And for that reason, most people see prophecy as foolishness. A man is not quick to get in touch with things he does not understand. They will listen to Donald Trump and take what he is saying to heart, but they think reading the Bible and praying for understanding is too hard.

Whereas God commands us to study.

> Study to shew thyself approved unto God, a workman that needed not to be ashamed, rightly dividing the word of truth. (2 Timothy 2:15)

When dealing with a problem, the word of God always comes to mind. I ask the Lord to order my steps and illuminate my path. I think about my brother-in-law, who tells me that God gave me a brain. And that is the thought of today's generation—the brain God gave us can guide us through everything.

Hebrew 11:6 says, "Without faith it is impossible to please God." So I weighed my circumstances. I genuinely believe the Lord called me as I completed my fifty years of studying the revelations, being seventy-nine and faced with health conditions.

I was exposed to beryllium at the Nevada Test Site, and for more than thirty years I incurred problems. The right side of my heart failed in 2012; the left lung became one-third filled with fluid; and the heart was beating at 10 percent capacity but is now functioning at 22 percent.

What is the most important thing we seek to accomplish down here as Christians?

The Lord blessed me to write this book under the said circumstances, and Jesus will bless it to be published.

Actions

What is God's people's primary source of service?

To go forth into the highways and byways and restrain man to come, and as the scriptures below say, I will perform it; I will keep Thy righteous judgment.

We, as followers of Christ, are committed that we will keep Thy righteous judgment and continue confirming the gospel.

We will follow the gospel! This is why we fight the devil—he is a liar—and we are placed in opposition to liars. This puts us in opposition to politicians, because they are mostly liars.

THE LORD TOLD US TO HAVE NO FELLOWSHIP WITH THE UNFAITHFUL WORKERS OF DARKNESS, BUT RATHER REPROVE THEM. (Ephesians 5:11)

Thy word is a lamp unto my feet, and a light unto my path. I Have sworn, and I will perform it, that I will keep thy righteous judgment. I am afflicted very much: quicken me, O Lord, according unto word. Accept, I beseech thee, the freewill offering of my mouth, O Lord, and teach me thy judgments. (Psalm 119:105–108)

Wrong Attitude

You, as Christians today, do improperly show your first concern, which is to see that things work to conform in a way to comply with society today. It has nothing to do with the will of God. That is not the Lord's will.

Judge not according to the appearance but judge righteous judgment. (John 7:24)

Now that is what we were sent by the Lord to do. We are fighting the devil, and we must stand up. The devil is controlling most of the Christian world by controlling the leadership. We, as Christians, must decide who we want to follow.

In the 2016 election, we followed the leadership of Jerry Lamon Falwell Jr. and voted for Donald Trump. On August 27, 2020, we saw that he had resigned from Liberty University.

Jerry Lamon Falwell Jr. was a teacher at the university and threw weekly "convocations"—gatherings that frequently featured Republican pundits and politicians. In place of what many Christian schools call "chapel," all on-campus students were required to attend hour-long meetings that included worship and a guest speaker. We sang songs about the power of the gospel, often followed by moving speeches about saving our country from socialists or protecting our borders from invading masses.

If we are following Christ, we must line up with the will and word of God. What we have been following is traditional church leadership, which involves politics.

Whereas we are in—counting the lying generation while writing this book. This generation was also struck by COVID-19, which the Lord suffered to get our attention.

Basic Foundation

Truth and proof at our beginning are our basic foundation and COVID-19. We can't separate COVID-19 from our beginning or from this book. Because of its effect on this world today, people all over the world are giving their lives to Christ. This is why we must involve COVID-19 in this book. It has an effect, which is worldwide, and in our attempt to win man to Christ, we must follow our foundation.

> Wisdom is the principal thing; therefore, get wisdom: and with all thy getting get understanding. (Proverbs 4:7)

> Then said Jesus to those Jews which believed on him, if ye continue in my word, then are ye my

disciples indeed. And ye shall know the truth, and
the truth shall make you free. (John 8:31–32)

We have not been seeking the truth. We have been simply following the instructions of our Christian leaders, who are following the
lobbyists and pushing the will of political leaders. This is why we have
been complaining about President Trump and his overreaching will.

But if I tarry long, that thou mayest know how
thou ought to believe thyself in the house of God,
which is the church of the living God, PILLAR,
and GROUND of the TRUTH. (1 Timothy 3:15)

That is the reason the truth is important to us.

The virus has brought frustrating and devastating circumstances
to our federal government, a totally new problem that no one knows
how to deal with, causing medical injuries and death. This problem
has placed our governors and mayors in a position of: What shall we
do? Besides that, the president has told them that it is their problem,
which makes it their problem to solve.

In prophecy, it is a major thing to deal with in leading someone
into the light. Our discussion on prophecy and the need therefore
shows that prophecy is not given out in step forms like 1-2-3 or A-B-
C. It was not the Lord's plan in so doing, which just left us to deal
with the situation confronting us. For myself, over the past fifty years
I was self-pushed into studying; now imagine that I'm writing a book
dealing with the two circumstances below.

In my fifty years of studying prophecy, I talked to many people
about it. I had shown my biblical interpretations to many, and one
of them told me that I should write a book on it.

When talking about it, I mentioned the flying roll, and my
family mentioned, "Why don't you write a book about that—the
flying roll?" I thought about it. I also thought about Evangelist Joyce
Meyers's book and the different struggles she had, but Jesus brought
her through.

And for a person like me, I am not a preacher, a Sunday school teacher, or anything like that, but I am certain that the Lord gave me the **interpretation** of revelations. I love the Lord, and I like studying the word.

Through the years, as I think of my experiences with the Lord, I think about the picture I drew as a child. I am attaching this as picture **A2**, which is me holding a Sunday school book involving the fourteenth chapter of the book of Revelation. I was a child, about five years old, looking at a Sunday school book, and the next second, I was behind the corner of a building, looking at an old man sharpening a sickle.

The old man said, "Come here." The old man is an angel sharpening the sickle. I refused to come because my thoughts were that he did not know I was there.

In the book, Jesus was coming up the road, and now he is even in the house, and the old man went out to talk with Jesus. I looked at Jesus from behind the building. While watching Jesus, the old man came again and was sharpening the sickle.

This time he called me, and I was out looking at the Lord. He never stopped sharpening the sickle or looked up, but said, "I will tell you what the Lord's will is for you." The next second, I was again outside of the book.

SUNDAY SCHOOL BOOK
THE FOURTEENTH CHAPTER OF REVELATION

I was a child about five or seven years old looking at a Sunday school book, and the next second I was behind the corner of the building, looking at an old man sharping a SICKLE

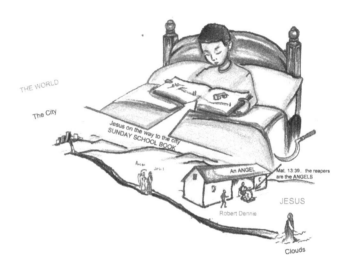

The old man said come here, the old man is the ANGEL sharping the sickle, I refuse to come because my thought was that he didn't know I was here.

Jesus Coming up the road, and now even with the house, and the old man went out to talk with Jesus, I looked at Jesus from behind the building, while watching Jesus the old man came again and was sharping the Sickle. This time he called me and I had to come out, he never stopped sharping the sickle or looked up, but said " I will tell you what the LORD'S WILL is for you" and at that second, I was again outside of the book.

This experience is one of the reasons I believe the Lord gave me the gift of understanding prophecy. I can remember the day of looking at that Sunday school book as if it happened yesterday. In studying prophecy, one can say it is **unintelligible**. And dealing with the lying generation.

13

In today's society, dealing President Trump

The news media is setting forth the position because of the approximately seventy-four million people who voted for President Trump. That large quantity of Trump's believers are saying that they believe that what Trump says is true.

There is no place in God's word that supports such a belief.

Foundational Truth and Our Access to Christ

Politicians make statements as they examine things.

1. They make statements, and when they hear or look at the statement, they do not like the way it is compared to the truth.
2. They are in an election and have made other statements, which do not all agree.
3. They have formed a group to support them in whatever way they become involved.
4. Or it could be President Trump, who believes he never makes a mistake or a lie.
5. "When we are liars, we attach ourselves to the devil, because he is a liar, and the father of it" (John 8:44).

Furthermore, truths and facts cannot be separated because it is impossible to connect "lies and facts." Therefore, we are setting forth truths and facts.

Truths and Facts

This book is found upon prophecy and man's destruction. It was the Lord God who made the call—the flying roll. We were created by the Lord, and we live under the will of God.

It was the Lord who destroyed the first world because of **sin**.

> And God looked upon the earth, and behold, it
> was corrupt; for all flesh had corrupted his way

upon the earth. And God said unto Noah, the
end of all flesh has become before me; for the
earth is filled with violence through them; and
behold, I will Destroy them with the earth.
(Genesis 6:12–13)

Now that we know God's dislike for sin, it will help us understand this prophecy and the Bible. As a new writer writing a book on prophecy and the Bible, this has me in a position of confusion. The only book I can find to give me some guidelines is *Writing Christian Fiction* by Jerry B. Jenkins.

With this understanding, I am seeking to do just the opposite—establish **proof** and **truth**. This is extremely difficult when you are living in a **lying generation**. And I say that it is a lying generation because we have a president who records a TV statement and the next day gives a recorded TV statement to the opposite.

The issue is that he has a 35 percent following of voters claiming that he "never lies," which forces us to confirm the proof and truth in everything (causing more work for us). Along with this fact, there are Bible scholars who have written books and taken positions that are not based on the truth.

Who knowing the judgment of God, that they
which commit such things are worthy of death,
not only do the same, but have pleasure in them
that do them. (Romans 1:32)

I am a member of the Sunrise Church in Rialto, California, and I love my church and pastor. I am including part of the sermon from March 8, 2020, because it fits in as a perfect part of this book.

We are evil people who must learn God. As we look at men of the past, we can also clearly see they were not perfect, but with their weaknesses, God still used them. AND IF WE COME TO HIM WITH A WILLING HEART, WALKING HONESTLY, AND WANTING TO SERVE HIM, HE WILL ALSO USE US.

We do not always see the value and necessity of things, but God teaches us through our waiting times. The great thing about knowing that God is all-powerful is understanding that even though you cannot see a solution to your problem, He can see it, and He is powerful enough to make it happen.

I know that in my life through the years, I have been confronted with numerous health issues—some with my heart and others with my lungs—but I was convinced that the Lord was going to work it out.

When someone tells you that the right side of your heart has failed (which means it's not working) and your left lung has 30 percent fluid, you certainly will not feel good about that news. Furthermore, my heart was pumping at 10 percent capacity. The thought that came into my mind was the word of God. The Lord told me, *I will never leave you. Call upon me in a time of trouble, and I shall deliver thee.*

I know the days for each of us are numbered, and when the end of your time comes, you can't get another second of grace.

I believe God has a plan for me in prophecy.

> For all have sinned and come short of the glory of God. (Romans 3:23)

> And the Lord spare unto Moses, saying. Speak unto the children of Israel, that they bring me an offering: of every man that giveth it willingly with his heart ye shall take my offering. (Exodus 25:1–2)

From the beginning, God has wanted to dwell with man to bring in his love and guidance. That is why God told them to build an altar to offer up man's sins, which would make it possible for man to reach God.

> And thou shall make an altar of shittim wood, five cubits long, and five cubits broad; the alter

shall be foursquare: and the high thereof shall be there three cubits. (Exodus 27:1)

In the tabernacle of the congregation without the vail, which is before the testimony, Aaron and his sons shall order it from the evening to morning before the Lord: it shall be a statute ever unto their generation on the behalf of the children of Israel. (Exodus 27:21)

Whereas we are evil people, God has opened a method of communication with us. Jesus gave his life for our salvation.

John bare witness of him, and cried, saying, this was he of whom I Speak, He that cometh after me is preferred before me: for he was before me. (John 1:15)

The next day John see Jesus coming unto him, and saith, Behold the Lamb of God which taketh away the sin of the world. (John 1:29)

And because truth and proof are important in the will of God and in the daily existence of our lives, establish truth and proof as the basis of study.

Actions

What is God's people's primary source of service?

O that my ways were directed to keep thy statutes. Then shall I not be ashamed, when I have respect unto all thy commandment. (Psalm 119:5–6)

We have sworn and committed to keeping the righteous judgment of God because we know that the vengeance of God is coming.

In flaming fire taking vengeance on them that know not God, and that obey not the gospel of our Lord Jesus Christ. (2 Thessalonians 1:8)

This is why we complain about today's Christian leadership—they are not obeying the Gospel of Christ. WE ARE IN THE LAST GENERATION.

1. There is no ministry today addressing a message for today's generation. By that, I mean addressing a message to the lying generation.
2. There are a lot of ministries that address their messages around the Old Testament.
3. Issues are involved in the Old Testament.

In today's generation, there are numerous killings of schoolchildren and teachers, all without a cause. The church leaders do not address the church in a manner to get rid of builders of rapid-fire weapons and stop the lobbyists from defending the weapon makers.

Issues of Today

It is impossible to do that without including politics, because politics play a particularly important role in our lives today. All aspects of our lives today are involved in politics.

Moving on to prophecy,

<<List contents sheet in this book, the illustrations are necessary.

a. Babylon= Religious apostasy/confusion
   Genesis 10:8–10
   Genesis 11:6–9
   Revelation 17:1–5
b. Beast= Kingdom, government, political power
   Daniel 7:23
c. Corrupt Woman= Corrupt, apostate church
   Ezekiel 16:15–58
   Ezekiel 23:2–21

Hosea 2:5

Hosea 3:1

d. Heads= major Powers, rulers, governments

> After this I beheld, and lo another, like a leopard, which had upon the back of it four wings of a fowl; the beast had also four heads; and dominion was given to it. (Daniel 7:6)

> Therefore the goat waxed very great: and when he was strong, the great horn was broken; and for it came up four notable ones toward the four winds of the heaven. (Daniel 8:8)

> And the rough goat are the king of Grecia: and the great horn that is between his eyes is the first king, (Rome). And here set forth are the kings that rose at Alexander's Death. (Daniel 8:21)

Empire 303 BC

Kingdom of Lysimachus

Kingdom of Cassander

Kingdom of Antigonus

Kingdom of Ptolemy

Kingdom of Seleucus

We now set forth the **mistaken fact** that, because there are biblical scholars who believe the Antichrist came out of one of the divisions of Alexander the Great's kingdom, we address the issue as follows.

Untrue Facts

Page facts further set forth that the Antichrist came out of one of the divisions of Alexander the Great's kingdom. This is NOT TRUE. Refer to document picture C, which is a one-page map of King

Alexander the Great's kingdom, "Division of Alexander's Empire, 303 BC." It indicates that Alexander's empire was divided among his five generals (which is not according to the scripture list 4).

To make facts clear, the four notable ones did not stand up to the four winds of heaven (at the death of King Alexander).

> Therefore the he goat waxed very great: and
> when he was strong, the great horn was broken;
> and for it came up four notable ones toward the
> four winds of the heaven. (Daniel 8:8)

This is TRUE. And that happened in a timeframe after the kingdoms of the five generals of King Alexander.

> And in the latter times of their kingdom, when
> the transgressors are come to full, a king of fierce
> countenance, and understanding dark sentences,
> shall stand up. (Daniel 8:23)

THAT REFERENCE IS MADE TO THE ANTICHRIST, WHO WOULD COME OUT OF ONE OF THE FOUR RISEN KINGDOMS. That would mean that the Antichrist came before Christ, which, according to the scriptures, "could not be true":

> I am come in my father's name, and you receive
> me not if another shall come in his own name
> him you will receive. (John 5:43)

So the fact is that prophecy cannot be found in false statements!

OVER 2500 YEARS AGO GOD NAMED EVERY 'WORLD GOVERNMENT FROM THE FIRST WORLD KINGDOM OF KING NEBUCHEDNEZZAR UNTIL

THE COMING KINGDOM OF CHRIST

Dan 1.5   Dan 2.37

Dan 2.38 King Nebuchadnezzar GOLD

GOLD   I

Dan 7.1 In the first year of Belshazzar

King of Babylon

King Darius of Media   King Cyrus of Persia

RAM   BRASS

King Caesar of Rome   IV

GOAT   IRON

King Alexander the Great

146 BC ROME crushed GREECE

THE COLOSSUS

THE FEET of the COLOSSUS

King Nebuchadnezzar

King Belshazzar

King Darius of Media

King Cyrus of Persia

Alexander the Great

King Caesar of Rome

King Alfred the Great

President Washington

Emperor of Russia

Emperor of Japan/China

BABY-LON | BABY-LON | MEDIA CYRUS | GREECE ROME | ENGLAND U.S.A | RUSSIA | JAPAN CHINA

THE BEAST   THE BEAST

ENGLAND

U.S.S.R.   U.S.A.

JAPAN CHINA

THE BEAST   THE BEAST

The Beast with SEVEN HEADS and TEN HORNS

This picture sets forth that King Nebuchadnezzar is the head of gold (we are not talking of the Babylonian Empire, but the king).

Today's Circumstances

We set forth the conditions in today's circumstances to make you aware of the problem caused by COVID-19 that the Lord suffered to be and to bring man's attention to Him.

On March 20, 2020, we were struggling with the virus. Today, there is a worldwide count of 275,00 people infected with the virus and 10,000 dead. In the USA, we have 13,479 infected and 196 dead.

Politics: Governors and Mayors Complain

Governors and mayors are on TV, doing everything they can to protect their states and cities. Some of them are constructing masks and making disinfectants to protect their states. Furthermore, they have said that within two or three weeks, they will run out of

1. masks,
2. surgical masks,
3. PPE gloves and mouth swabs,
4. beds, and
5. ventilators.

Governors and Mayors Request

Where is the federal government?

So it is impossible today not to include politics, which involves the **truth** and **proof.**

The president knew about the virus in January—January first or no later than January 10—yet he made no effort to go forth as our president in preparing to provide for us.

What he was doing was talking. Constant talk about the virus was being done by the Democrats to give him a black eye (playing down the virus).

It was not until March that he began to face the reality that the virus was real. He let approximately two months pass without doing anything to protect us. Now the governors and mayors are complaining.

Circumstances

Pandemic experts issue sobering warnings about the future. Pandemic experts John Barry and Marc Lasith co-authored a new report predicting that the coronavirus pandemic could last up to two more years. They're warning that things could get considerable worse than what we've seen so far. (CNN US)

This is an industrious country. We build things, and it is my position that our president should be acting like a president and building something—like masks, beds, ventilators, and other medical supplies needed. Trump should have ordered factories to manufacture the necessary medical supplies, beds, and ventilators.

The billionaires are contributing millions toward helping with the virus. Mr. Henning and Frieden told us that while the nonprofit and philanthropic sectors can often move more quickly and flexible than large governments, their role is to fill in the gaps, not to compensate for government inaction.

The governor of Florida said, "We need to manufacture." Mayor de Blasio blamed the president for the looming supplies. Looking at existing critical circumstances, it is evident that we must consider our choices in politics because our survival depends on them.

Christians Believers

Most believers do not address themselves on a one-on-one basis when choosing a political candidate. I want to thoroughly establish the fact that in today's world, we must include politics. Our daily lives depend on our political leaders. We are in fear of destruction because the existing coronavirus will destroy us.

Why are they listing the leaders of Christian organizations? Here is an example of what the Christian leaders are doing.

In the 2016 election, we followed the leadership of Jerry Lamon Falwell Jr. and voted for Donald Trump. On this day, August 27, 2020, we see that he has resigned from Liberty University.

Jerry Lamon Falwell Jr. was a teacher at the university and yet threw weekly "convocations"—gatherings that frequently featured Republican pundits and politicians. In place of what many Christian schools call "chapel," all on-campus students were required to attend an hour-long meeting that included worship and a guest speaker. We sang songs about the power of the gospel, often followed by moving speeches about saving our country from socialists or protecting our borders from invading masses.

Based on these facts, we should stop following such Christian leaders.

The USA is a large country, and in its growth, the existing political parties have set forth an example of how they operate. Giving us a choice between the Democrat, Republican, or Libertarian, the Democrat Party is more liberal than the Republican Party; by that, we mean they will support funds for needy organizations. Therefore, those of us with above-average incomes choose to be Republicans.

In dealing with political parties, they are often supported and involved with organizations. In setting forth that point, it is not just man's political decision about politics and the different groups on radio, which includes mobile, radio, and television, with other news agencies' MANIPULATION to control the country and world issues.

I know as I look at Russia, that Putin has a plan for the future of total dictatorship for all world rulers, including the USA, and he has worked across Europe as well at employing his plan.

And I would like to see more Christian brothers and sisters be given the opportunity to see and know more about the prophecy (with revelations scholars help, that is what TV shows should be doing).

Because I have been studying revelations for fifty years and the things that I've learned, I have been encouraged to be more diligent in serving God. I know that if you were studying as I am, it would encourage you as well.

Furthermore, I am seventy-nine years old, and I am writing this book. As I have never done anything like this before, I realize this is a major undertaking, particularly with my health conditions, but I am determined to complete this project.

Thoughts about the *flying roll*, and no one having set it forth, with the actions today about our young generation has rejected Christ, and so many people today are joining organizations built upon hate and going forth killing because of that organization.

I am disturbed by what I hear on the news. You know when it comes to Christian organizations, you know how they are going to vote, and my thoughts on those Christian organizations are prophetic.

President Trump has three million dollars in a Chinese bank account. You, as Trump supporters, have provided that three million in his bank account. And Christian community, that was poor Christians giving to your service, the money you gave. The Lord knows that you are knowledgeable about the will and word of God.

> Who knowing the judgment of god, that they which commit such things are worthy of death, not only do the same, but have pleasure in them that do so. (Romans 1:32)

Actions

What is God's people's primary source of service?

> Thy word is a lamp unto my feet, and a light unto my path. I Have sworn, and I will perform it, that I will keep thy righteous judgment. I am afflicted very much: quicken me, O Lord, according to thy word. Accept, I beseech thee, the freewill offering of my mouth, O Lord, and teach me thy judgments. (Psalm 119:105–108)

THE TRUE FOLLOWERS OF GOD KNOW AND BELIEVE THE WORD OF GOD, AND THEY KNOW THAT HIS VENGEANCE IS COMING.

> In flaming fire taking vengeance on them that know not God, and that obey not the gospel of our Lord Jesus Christ. (2 Thessalonians 1:8)

The church has refused to stand on the value of truth, in the past and today, whereas the church is supposed to be the pillar of truth. (Keeping in mind that God destroyed the first world because

25

of sin.) And today's organizations are built upon hate, want to kill and generate fear, and have given no thought to the fact that God destroyed the first world.

And today, His attitude hasn't improved any better toward hateful attitudes or those participants therein. And we are under attack by a virus that has the world under siege. And people all over the world are giving their lives to Christ. The reason I say that the virus has this world under siege is because its attack seems to be similar to that of a military state synonym (control of things). At this point, no matter which direction science takes, we are not getting the results we need. It is as if we are fighting some type of force.

> Then said Jesus to those Jews which believed on him, if ye continue in my word, then are ye my disciples indeed. And ye shall know the truth, and the truth shall make you free. Which is why we take a hard stand on truth, because the weapons of our warfare are not carnal, but mighty though God to the pulling down of strong holds. (John 8:31–32)

> But if I tarry long, that thou mayest know how thou ought to believe thyself in the house of God, which is the church of the living God, PILLAR, and GROUND of the TRUTH. (I Timothy 3:15)

The devil is beating Christians to death. In the past two hundred years, they have produced a prejudice-killing generation of Christians with no thought about where they are going to spend eternity. IT IS A HURTFUL THING TO THINK THAT OUR CHRISTIAN GENERATION DOES NOT CARE ABOUT THEIR CHILDREN.

FOR EXAMPLE, WHITE NATIONALIST CARE NOTHING ABOUT HEAVEN. They only care about "hate." Keep this in mind: We are not fighting the White Nationalists; we are fighting the devil. He has given them the thought that "hate is more important than salvation," and their family members who are in the church have the first responsibility to reach out to them. And as we examine them, it appears that they are the offspring of the Christian body, and that is why we say today's Christians care nothing about their children—White Nationalists' children—because according to their actions, for all eternity, hell will be their home. (My thoughts are, *Once they get to hell, are they still thinking of hate?* Because they have all eternity to think about it.) WHILE THEY FIGHT TO PROTECT THE CHILDREN IN THE WOMB, "THEY CARE NOTHING ABOUT THE ONE THEY PUSHED OUT."

> But if any provide not for his own, and especially for those of his own house, he hath denied the faith and is worse than an infidel. (1 Timothy 5:8)

We must also consider that the Lord is the same yesterday, today, and forever more.

Pharaoh, the Egyptian, was evil to a state that God hardened his heart, which means He could not change. Exodus 7:3 says, "And I will harden Pharaoh heart."

Man can become evil to the point that God will harden His heart, which means hell will be man's home.

> Jesus Christ the same yesterday, and today, and forever. (Hebrews 13:8)

There are some who would say that what I am saying is hard, but often, the truth is hard, and after the flying roll goes forth, there is no forgiveness.

We are the last generation; "the fulfillment of God's plan of anger with sin will fall upon this generation." We know that God destroyed the first world because of a hating and killing generation.

> Take no part in unfruitful works of darkness. (Ephesians 5:11)

(If you are a liar, then you know where you're going.)

The devil is not asleep; he is sending forth a message to control the mind of man! You should take no part in unfruitful works of darkness.

> Who knowing the judgment of God, that they
> which commit such things are worthy of death,
> not only do the same, but have pleasure in them
> that do so. (Romans 1:32)

Furthermore, in Evangelist Joyce Meyer's book's (*Battlefield of the Mind*) section, "Delivery from Mind-Binding Spirits," nearly every deliverance God has brought to me has been progressive and has come about by believing and confessing the word of God. John 8:31–32 and Psalm 107:20 are my testimony. In John 8:31–32, Jesus says, "If you abide in My word…you are truly My disciple. And you will know the Truth, and the Truth will set you free."

The will and word of the Lord must also be considered. And why are the said facts important? No one is paying attention to understanding what the **word and will of God are.**

We must take to heart that God loves us, and because of his love, he opens a path to connect with us. **Jesus died for our sins.**

I saw a picture on the news. They were showing the picture of a man who lived on the street. He was on his knees, praising God, and a newsperson asked him, "Why are you praising God? You have nothing, and you're living on the street."

The man answered, "I have salvation, the greatest gift of all."

That event grabbed my attention because I've talked to people in my life. Some are wealthy, and others are extremely intelligent. But to my understanding, they are ignorant and unseeing. They seek to evaluate things according to their understanding and have no patience to look at the ways and will of God.

> Therefore if a man be in Christ, he is a new crea-
> ture: old things are passed away; behold, all things

are become new. And all things are of God, who
has reconciled us to himself by Jesus Christ, and
hath given into us the ministry of reconciliation.
(2 Corinthians 5:17–21)

The facts are all my saved life; we were striving to accomplish that very thing, "that which COVID-19 has accomplished." Furthermore, it has been set forth that all around the world, people are giving their lives to Christ—a blessing—because these are the last days, and man should be giving attention to the Lord and His word.

And to you who are troubled rest with us, when
the Lord Jesus shall be revealed from heaven with
his mighty angles. In flaming fire taking vengeance on them that know not God, and that
obey not the gospel of our Lord Jesus Christ. (2
Thessalonians 1:7–8)

Man's desires are to do his own will. Man wants things his own way—the easy one. It's hard to get men to read/study the Bible. It is my desire to reach out to all mankind with the true word of God. We're seeking to protect His eternal soul.

Even the Spirit of truth; whom the world could
not receive, because it sees him not, neither know
him; for he dwelleth with you, and shall be in
you. (John 14:17)

(And we pray and wait to hear from the spirit of truth.)

Revelations

I have set about talking to family members and friends about the Bible, and there are many of them who do not believe that the knowledge of the revelations is important to them.

They tell me that the revelations are not important for salvation, which I confess is true, but it led us to the question of **the flying roll**. WHEN GOD WILL SEND FORTH A CURSE ACROSS THE FACE OF THE EARTH, that is the time when the knowledge of revelations is important to your very salvation, which is why we are seeking to inform you.

Illustrations must be attached for clarification.

Clarification Illustrations

List the names of the kings and the kingdoms, beginning with King Nebuchadnezzar, the first-world king. And list each of the following world kingdoms in the order in which they arose, showing the names God gave the kingdoms.

Defining the Names of the Kingdoms

This is why prophecy is important—we serve an all-knowing God, a God who explains things to us and can have set this up in a 1-2-3 and/or A-B-C order, but he did not choose to do so. And we are not about to question Him. One person questioned God—Job. And God answered Job.

> Then the Lord answered Job out of the whirlwind and spoke. (Job 38:1)
>
> Where west thou when I laid the foundation of the earth? (Job 38:4)

Looking at the Lord's answer to Job, I don't believe I want to question Him about anything because I know that part of His word is study.

> Study to shew thyself approved unto God, a workman that need not to be ashamed, rightly dividing, the word of truth. (2 Timothy 2:15)

It's terrible when we have people who don't want to study, but salvation is worth it. I cannot give up because He told me to go into the highways and byways and restrain men from coming, and writing this book is in part my way of going.

Furthermore, the Lord set forth in revelations what the end events would be.

It is necessary to introduce you to some facts—facts involving end-time prophecy (this will establish a point in time for the prophecy). To establish proof, the last four nations of man now exist— England, the USA, the USSR, and Japan/China.

To establish that point in time, it is necessary to display numerous revelation issues and facts, which is why I can see why numerous biblical scholars haven't gone forward with such revelation books.

And through the years, I have noticed that there are Bible scholars out there, and I have noticed and followed every TV show where different scholars set forth prophecy presentations. There is only one problem I have, which is that of all the TV shows, there was not one show or program.

That was prophecy, starting 2,500 years ago with King Nebuchadnezzar as the first-world king and following the step-by-step change of each world kingdom up to today. This is exactly what our prophecy does, including pictures and scriptural instructions.

Revelation is a part of a Vision. That is what I stand for.

> And the Lord answered me, and said, Write the vision, and make it plain upon tables, that he may run that read it. For the vision is yet for an appointed time, but at the end it shall speak, and not lie though it tarry, wait for it; because it will surely come, it will not tarry…but the just shall live by faith. (Habakkuk 2:2–4)

God is giving us revelational instructions through His word. God gave man knowledge of the rise of all world governments. The Lord gave King Nebuchadnezzar the name of all world kingdoms, starting 2,500 years ago, his being the first.

But there is a God in heaven that reveals secrets,
and make known to the King Nebuchadnezzar
what shall be in the last days. (Daniel 2:28)

God gave Nebuchadnezzar a dream that troubled him. He could not sleep or rest at all, so he called all his wise men, told them the problem, and ordered them to correct the problem by telling him his dream and giving him the interpretation.

And if they could not do so, they would be killed and their homes destroyed. All the wise men of Babylon sought out Daniel, who, with his followers, desired mercy from the God of heaven. God gave Daniel the interpretation of the dream. Daniel asked to see the king and explained the dream given by God.

There are also documents attached to this book.

Prophecy Illustrations

Colossus (picture A)—this picture illustrates the name of the world kingdoms up to the broken horn, the time of the gentiles.

a. This event set forth the complete history of the times of the gentiles.
b. Starting with King Nebuchadnezzar, at the very top is the head of gold, and the second kingdom is silver, that of King Belshazzar of Babylon, who was King Nebuchadnezzar's grandson.
c. And the third kingdom is that of the ram, which is King Darius of Media and King Cyrus of Persia.
d. And the next kingdom is the goat, which is King Alexander the Great. That goat has a horn, which is Rome, "and that is a fact we will prove."
e. And the next kingdom is the feet.

After this I saw in the night visions, and behold
a fourth beast, dreadful and terrible, and strong
exceedingly; and it had great iron teeth: it

devoured and brake in pieces and stamped the residue with the feet of it: and it was diverse from all the beasts that were before it; and it had ten horns. (Daniel 7:7)

(The fourth beast is shown in picture M.)

And when we look at the picture, we see "the beast" listing four nations, which are

a. England
b. USA
c. USSR
d. Japan/China

Now we have listed all the world kingdoms, and set forth that the prophecy of God is proven true by world history. That document set forth dates and scriptures.

Page C—one-page map titled "King Alexander as the Great Horn That Was Broken: Division of Alexander's Empire 303 BC" shows the five divisions of Alexander's kingdom to his five generals.

1. Kingdom of Lysimachus
2. Kingdom of Cassander
3. Kingdom of Antigonus
4. Kingdom of Ptolemy
5. Kingdom of Seleucus

Information: Alexander the Great as the great horn that was broken, document facts—NOT TRUE.

Sitting Forth Errors

1. According to Daniel 8:8, "Therefore the He Goat waxed very Great and when he was strong the Great Horn was Broken, and for it came up four Notable Ones Toward the

four Winds of HEAVEN." (The facts are that five horns came up for Alexander's generals, which ruled at his death.)

2. Furthermore, those five horns are not divided toward the four winds of HEAVEN.

3. Further proof: "The statement is that the Antichrist would have to come out of one of the divisions of Alexander's kingdom" (which is not true). That would mean the Antichrist came before Christ. This is NOT TRUE. Refer to the verses below.

I am come in my father's name, and you receive me not if another shall come in his own name him you will receive. (John 5:43)

There are only four divisions according to prophecy. (Daniel 8:8)

4. The Antichrist came out of one of the five divisions of King Alexander's kingdoms (NOT TRUE according to Daniel 8:8).

5. According to John 5:43, "I am come in my father's name, and you receive me not if another shall come in his own name him you will receive." Jesus clearly made it understood that he comes FIRST.

6. a. It is clearly stated that King Belshazzar is in the silver kingdom.
   b. As this prophecy displays, Media and Persia are the brass kingdoms.

7. When Daniel interrupted King Nebuchadnezzar's dream, it was made clear that King Nebuchadnezzar was the head of gold and not the Babylonian Empire.

8. Daniel 2:37 says, "Thou O King art a King of Kings."

Based upon the said facts, it is clearly understood that King Alexander the Great was not the broken horn, which keeps this prophecy in proper order. This prophecy is found in an action of earthly events, and we must establish the truth and proof as the basis of the study (because we are the lying generation).

I need to define the term **media/truth** because it is important to understand it for the entire book. While traveling in our cars with our radios on, there are radio show speakers and other organizers who have prepared information to give us, which is **false media**. Stating that fact, we are now going to proceed.

Truth and Proof

So because of the problems occurring in this generation, we must address the issues occurring in this generation. I am setting forth points that must be understood prior to confronting "truth and proof" as the basis of the study.

With respect to politics and the president (to prevent you from being controlled by mind-binding spirits), he has a 35 percent following of voters who claim that he "never lies." This forces us to confirm the proof and truth in everything. We would have fewer problems writing this book if we weren't addressing the "35% of voters claiming that he never lies." We could not complete this book, living in a lying generation, without addressing those issues.

Joyce Meyers carefully and elaborately details the issues of the mind, so while reading it, I could see that people living in this generation of lies could benefit from reading and understanding this book. This is why we are recommending that those who do not have the book buy one. It will make it much easier to understand our book of prophecy.

This world is confronted with an extremely new and unbelievable problem—a **virus** that came from Wuhan, China, and no one knows exactly how people became affected by it. We must mention our president again because he is still the president and the chief person in charge of leading this country.

The facts are that the virus was first detected approximately on the first of January or January tenth, and for approximately two months, the president took no action to take steps to protect the country from the virus.

As discussion of the virus began, several governors began to address the issues of the virus, and it appears that the hardest-hit state was New York. Governor Andrew Cuomo went into action, setting up as many test facilities as possible at the time.

In New York, Ann Sucks-Berg and Northwell Hearth came forth, declaring that "retired doctors and nurses are coming forward to help." The governor said that forty to eighty thousand people would be tested. In New York, 10,000 people have been infected by the virus. If the president does not push testing, more people will die.

Red Rooster Restaurant was feeding five hundred people a day. Senator Kristen Gilbert pushes the Senate to vote on the sweeping Ecopoetic Bill, which is terrible for New York as it needs more money.

Governor Cuomo says cases double every six days. Firefighters in New York have tested positive. The governor states that we have 53,000 ventilators, and we need 140,000. Ventilators are our biggest critical need as the peak looms.

Hospital systems in New York saw a 10 percent increase. They need more help than the bill is giving them. According to the *New York Times*, in the article "At War with No Ammo," the lack of proper masks, gowns, and eye gear is imperiling the ability of medical workers to fight the coronavirus—and putting their own lives at risk.

New York Hospital is facing a deluge of cases, and WHO, US, could become the **epicenter** of a global outbreak. New York has 26,300 cases of COVID-19. Governor Andrew Cuomo warns of a rapid influx. New York intends to test cases two to three weeks away.

New York "On Pause" Governor Cuomo Executive Order

People under seventy should limit outdoor activity.
Restrictions on the elderly and those with underlying medical conditions
Nonessential business gatherings of any size are banned.
Nonessential businesses must be kept closed.
Essential businesses can remain open.

The New York governor reports that we have 53,000 ventilators, and we need 140,000. The president must do something. People will die without ventilators, one of the hospital doctors stated with their COVID-19 patients. Once their conditions reach the stage where they need a ventilator, you have minutes to get it to them.

Let's go back to politics and the president (to prevent you from being controlled by mind-blinding spirits). In tucking issues of things occurring today and politics, we must observe some of the circumstances by which this president became president.

1. He does not make good decisions; he is a liar.
2. He returns to the decision and changes it.
3. He makes a recorded statement about what he intends to do with an issue.
4. He then returns and tells you that you did not understand what he said in his recorded statements.
5. He said on *Fox Business*, "You know, in April, supposedly, it dies with the hotter weather" (he is speaking of the coronavirus).
6. On February 24, he baselessly claimed that the situation was "under control."
7. On February 25, a senior White House official falsely claimed the virus had been "contained."

Now our position is that the surgeon general has stated that the COVID-19 outbreaks will be worse in New Orleans, Detroit, and Chicago, while Governor Cuomo states that his cases will double every three days.

With the understanding of all the things said above, the president's aids state that the president is itching to scale back "social distancing after fifteen days." The president himself came on TV and confirmed that fact. The said facts confirm my statement above that "the president makes statements and then changes his mind." That causes confusion.

The fact is that the president states that the governors and mayors should be responsible in their states. But it is also a fact that, as president, he has a responsibility toward the country, which for approximately two months he failed to perform.

Define **responsibility**. It is the state of fact of having a duty to deal with something or having control over someone. It is the state of being held accountable for something. "A true leader takes responsibility for their team and helps them achieve goals."

That is the problem we have today. There is no leadership coming from the top, and we are confronted with a major problem. The governors, the next level down, have been told it is their problem, and the top level is giving them no help.

The president was asked what his rating was for his position of caring for the country. He said a ten. Keeping track of our concern for the truth, the president counting himself as a ten is a lie. I repeat that two months passed, and he did nothing to protect the country.

The issues set before you are for the purpose of preventing yourself from being bound by mind-blinding spirits. It can be done by following the Gospel of Christ, the word of God, and truth.

We must stay mindful that the devil is not asleep. He is a liar and the father of a lie, which is one of his main methods of attack. When dealing with a person who is a lair, we should not just line up with whatever that person says. We should examine them and their statements for the truth.

There is a reason a person lies, and you can be sure it is not for the purpose of righteousness. Jesus is the word. Jesus is truth and righteousness. For sure, if we are not following righteousness, then we are following the path of the devil. (Trump's functions are identical to Satan's.)

We're not saying that the president is following the path of the devil, but the fact is that President Trump settled a lawsuit against him. It was reported in *NBC News* by Tom Winter and Detrusor Clark that the federal court approved a $25 million Trump settlement on Tuesday with students who said they were duped by Donald Trump and his now-defunct Trump University, which promised to teach them the "secret of success" in the real estate industry. No one gives away $25 million to people if they are not lying and cheating.

Decade in the Red: Trump Tax Figures Show
Over $1 Billion in Business Losses

Newly obtained tax information reveals that
from 1985 to 1994, Donald J. Trump's businesses
were in far bleaker condition than was previously
known. (Russ Buettner and Susanne Craig, *New
York Times*, May 8, 2019)

By the time his master-of-the-universe memoir "Trump: The
Art of the Deal" hit bookstores in 1987, Donald J. Trump was
already in deep financial distress, losing tens of millions of dollars on
troubled business deals, according to previously unrevealed figures
from his federal income tax returns.

The numbers show that in 1985, Mr. Trump reportedly lost
$46.1 million from his core businesses—largely casinos, hotels, retail
spaces, and buildings. They continue to lose money every year, total-
ing $1.17 billion in losses for the decade.

In the hotels that Mr. Trump built in 1985, did he pay his bills
to the contractors who did the construction?

Hundreds allege Donald Trump does not pay his
bills, June 9, 2016, landed a $400,000 contract
to build the bases for slots machines, registra-
tion desks, bars, and other cabinets at Harrah's at
Trumps. (*USA Today*)

Trump still owes money to contractors who built Taj Mahal
casino on January 24, 2020, and what he did not tell the sources of
contractors who worked on casino was that he could not pay their
bills (NorthJersey.com).

Donald Trump's business plan left a trail of
unpaid bills. (*The Wall Street Journal*, June 9,
2016)

Trump's best-known payments dispute was in Atlantic City in the early 1990s, when Trump executives told contractors, when working for Donald Trump, he does not pay his bills. (*USA Today*)

Trump D.C. hotel contractors say they are owed millions. (NPR, January 11, 2017)

Existing Conditions

Man refuses to believe what he cannot understand—in most cases. And we are fighting an enemy that has been on the battlefield for a long time, "the devil," and he knows that.

That is why most of the devil's followers deal with lies, games, and confusion. Confusion gives them control over things.

God's people must comply with

But let him ask in faith, nothing weaving. For he that wavered is like a wave of the sea driven with the wind and tossed. (James 1:6)

A double mined man is unstable in all his ways. (James 1:8)

Christian Believers Judging Themselves

Today, Christian believers are judging themselves. You can be looking at believers for five, ten, or fifteen years, looking at circumstances and situations affecting this nation and the world, and thinking, *I know that I am a believer because I work at the church and give to the church.*

At the same time, I am not stupid. I know that some of the things set forth by the companies or people we support are not right. But I know the Lord will understand because I am a Christian (NOT TRUE).

It is in circumstances such as this that the flying roll is being sent forth. The Lord does not want us to support or do the wrong things.

> That we henceforth be no more childrens, tossed to and fro and carried about with every wind of doctrine, by the sleige of men, and cunning crafti-ness, whereby they lie to deceive. (Ephesians 4:14)

This is a battle we cannot wage effectively if we always try to come across the world as merely nice, nonchalant, docile, and agree-able people.

We must not take our cues from people who are perfectly happy to compromise the truth whenever possible. Friendly dialogue may sound pleasant, but neither Christ nor the apostles ever agreed with soul-destroying error by building collegial relations with false teach-ers. In fact, we are expressly forbidden to do so (Romans 16:17; 2 Corinthians 6:14–15; 2 Thessalonian 3:6; 2 Timothy 3:5).

Speaking of Christians, make deals with President Trump because he has promised to shut down abortion clinics, and help in that manner.

The Christian community is now standing in full support of Trump, with all his lying and cheating people, supporting White racism, and a large number of his friends indicted and found guilty of crimes.

Furthermore, President Trump instructed his followers to come to the Capitol Building on January 6 and stand up for him, or they were going to lose their country.

The scripture is clear about how we are to respond when the very foundation of the Christian faith is under attack.

1. Work out salvation (God is bound to truth).
   We can tell which position stands for truth.

   > Prove all things; hold fast that which is good. (1 Thessalonians 5:21 KJV)

A faithful witness will not lie: But a false witness will utter lies. (Proverbs 14:5 KJV)

2. Avoid a confused mind.
   I know that you are truthful and explain to your church friends and leaders that you hear their decisions, but you also want to pray on the matter and see how the Holy Ghost leads you. That will avoid confusion, and, possibly, the Holy Ghost has explained a different plan to you.

3. Bring a spiritual mind or conscience.
   Until we become spirit-conscious, we will not be able to understand what God is saying to our spirit. Spiritual things will be indistinct. But the more spirit-conscious we become, the more real the leading of the Lord will be to us. We need to think of ourselves as spiritual beings, processing souls, and living in bodies.

I am seventy-nine years old, and I have learned that it is important to deal with issues as they present themselves—when they are particularly important issues.

Unfortunately, the Christian church will consistently be an organization looked up to by the world for influence. And that is a problem for us because that places the church in a position whereby it must stand on the value of truth.

Actions

What are God's people's primary source of service?

Thy word is a lamp unto my feet, and a light unto my path. I Have sworn, and I will perform it, that I will keep thy righteous judgment. I am afflicted very much: quicken me, O Lord, according unto thy word. Accept, I beseech thee,

the freewill offering of my mouth, O Lord, and
teach me thy judgments. (Psalm 119:105–108)

THEY ARE NOT ALLOWING THE WORD OF GOD
TO GUIDE THEM, BUT THEY ARE LISTENING TO
THE MEDIA. CHRISTIANS TODAY ARE NOT CON-
CERNED ABOUT WHAT GOD'S PEOPLE'S PRIMARY
SOURCE OF SERVICE SHOULD BE. (Church leadership
today should be a concern.) Not about media in this world today
because media is an influencing factor and there are large organiza-
tions in control of the media (all evil concerns).

What Christians should be concerned about is a world issue—coal.

Thy word is a lamp unto my feet, and a light
unto my path. (Psalm 119:105)

The US coal industry in this nation was the first industry to
supply the nation's need for primary heating. Of course, there has
always been gas, but coal was primary. The coal industry spent a
large amount of money to obtain and produce coal. Over time, the
air quality was damaged by the coal. It created a problem that needed
to be addressed.

Lobbyist

The states with the largest coal power stations in the US—
Georgia, Indiana, Michigan, and Virginia—suffered because of the
loss of the coal industry. Businesses fail throughout the city and state,
as several family generations have worked in the industry.

People losing their businesses and their homes with no direction to turn can give us an understanding as to why there are so many
areas of complaint today.

THIS IS WHY POLITICIANS CANNOT BE
TRUSTED; THIS IS ONE OF THE REASONS WE
ADDRESS THE "MEDIA/TRUTH."

As we stop and think about it, we cannot move this world back in time to pump up coal production and use it in this nation again. But if I am a politician and want to be elected, this is what I will tell those states I am going to do—media/truth.

Oil came forth as the second industry to supply the nation's need for primary heating. The oil we needed was not all in this country but had to be imported. Sometimes there were problems with transporting the oil over the ocean, plus the oil caused greenhouse gases.

There were accidents with some of the ships while transporting the oil, which caused millions of gallons of oil to be dumped into the ocean, which required a major cleanup process.

Nuclear power plants are working with dangerous products because there have been accidents in different places around the world, which also require the need for lobbyists.

I thought it was necessary to set forth events that show the need for lobbyists because those lobbyists are the people we are referring to when we mention people on radio programs as well as people on TV shows, giving you information to control your opinion about this nation and world issues, media, and truth.

> Study to shew thyself approved unto God, a workman that needed not to be ashamed, rightly dividing the word of truth. (2 Timothy 2:15)

> Wherefore, my beloved, as ye have always obeyed, not as in my presence only, but now much more in my absence, work out your own salvation with fear and trembling. (Philippians 2:12)

> For though we walk in the flush, we do not war after flush: For the weapons of our warfare are not carnal, but mighty though God to the pulling down of strong holds. (2 Corinthians 3:3–4)

Doubt is a choice. Such areas as this are why I mention *Battlefield of the Mind*. I read the book, and if you had also, you would be in a better position mentally to deal with this situation.

Often your church brothers and sisters will call, telling you maybe we should discuss this, a lot of people are talking, we want to be sure we do the right thing.

As men and women of God we must commit ourselves to a faithful stand on truth:

There is no need to be dealing with doubt and confused mind, as a man or woman of God, when we have prayed and waited to hear from the Holy Spirit, you stand upon your faith.

A true work of the Holy Spirit convicts the heart of sin, combats worldly lusts, and cultivates spiritual fruit in the lives of Gods people.

I the Holy Spirit cultivates fruit in your lives:

> Take no part in unfruitful works of darkness. (Ephesians 5:11)

(A false witness utters lies.)

> Trust in the Lord with all thine heart; and lean not unto thine own understanding. In all thy ways acknowledge him, and he shall direct thy path. (Proverbs 3:5–6)

The Response of Faithful Christians

As we said earlier, we must pray and wait for the response from the Holy Ghost when making decisions on issues we need to resolve. The importance of fighting for truth emerges as a dominant factor when seeking to serve Jesus.

> But ye believe, build up yourself on your Holy Faith, praying in the Holy Ghost. Keeping yourselves in the love of God, looking for the mercy of your Lord Jesus Christ unto eternal life. (Joel 1:20–21)

The Christian martyr throughout history stood for truth. As a point in time, you can examine this entire book, looking at Donald Trump's entire history of abuse.

Jesus and His apostles were not terrorists or violent people, but they fought for truth by proclaiming it in the face of fierce opposition and refusing to renounce or forsake the truth no matter what threats were made against them.

> That good thing was committed unto thee keep by the Holy Ghost which dwelled in us. (2 Timothy 1:14)

Furthermore, today we must understand that we live in an intelligent world, and the devil has not retired. THERE ARE PEOPLE AND ORGANIZATIONS WORKING WITH THE INTENT OF CONTROLLING YOUR MIND AND GIVING YOU FALSE INFORMATION IN ORDER TO GUIDE YOU.

This Bible prophecy interpretation must confront all "world issues."

I have a brother-in-law, and we spend time together. He is a very loving and giving person. At times, we discuss the will and word of God. He believes that many preachers are just trying to get people's money.

So I ask him, "What about the salvation of your soul?" He says his salvation can be decided by the Lord at judgment time. I ask him if he has received Jesus as his personal savior. He says no. He does not believe he needs to. His feelings are that he is going to wait for the judgment because he knows that he is a good person and believes that Jesus will receive him. I cannot tell him he is wrong. I can't judge him, but my feelings are that I'm grateful for Jesus dying for me, because there is no way I want to trust my eternal salvation in the judgment.

I am not saying that I am a terrible person because I am not, but I know that by passing this way, I did something wrong, and I thank Jesus for forgiving me. I thank Him for my eternal salvation.

And I am one who studies the Bible, and I have read what my savior says about us.

> Yea, thou hardest not; yea thou newest not; yea from the time that thine ear was not opened: for I knew that thou wildest deal very treacherously and was called a transgressor from the whom. (Isaiah 48:8)

(That is a long-time **transgressor**.)

In my study of the revelations, I am troubled by my loved ones and close friends when I do not get a breakthrough in knowing they have received Christ as their personal savior. With all the things I can see and know, I do not know why it does not matter to some people.

> We should know from God's word that we should study the word, and its only though study and prayer, we would grow in the word. (2 Timothy 2:15)

> No man that warmth entangled himself with the affairs of this life; that he may please him who hath chosen him to be a soldier. (2 Timothy 2:4)

> Consider what I say, and the Lord gives understanding in all things. (2 Timothy 2:7)

Considering first that men do not want to study the word and that it is only through prayer and study that man can receive God's blessings, "The Lord gives you understanding in all things."

We need to pray and ask the Lord to help us and give us the desire to study the word in Jesus's name. Starting off in this sinful world, without Christ in your life, we are treacherous, and west called a transgressor from whom?

WE ARE IN THE ENTRY, STARTING REVELA-
TIONS. And soon, THE **FLYING ROLL.**

The flying roll is a curse the Lord will send upon wicked and
self-judging Christians. While judging themselves, they see no problem
because they attend church, help in church, and say that all is well (not
true). But while living in this sinful world, they cannot become partak-
ers with the lobbyists while supporting their effort to accomplish their
end, and the lobbyists leave no end unturned.

You Need to Be Delivered from Mind-Blinding Spirits

The devil's work is treacherous, with thoughts deceiving you
into believing that you are only supporting the wicked operation and
not performing it, which is nothing wrong. (Mistake, that is wrong.)

Furthermore, when Christian brothers and sisters sit and talk
together, you are comfortable, but while the devil is coming against
your mind, he knows that if he can control your thoughts, then he
has control over you. This is where Joyce Meyer's book, *Battlefield of
the Mind*, will guide you.

You do not consider the hold the devil has on this world today.
There are children in our society who are going into schools and killing adults and children. Furthermore, there are hate groups going to
churches and murdering as many as possible without a cause. There
are hate groups that assemble and murder people without a cause.

This day, man removes himself from God's truth. The influence
of the Lord's Spirit, the mercy of His grace, and evil's own motive are
sufficient to guarantee their doom. As men and women of God, we
need to set aside time to observe our children, wherein we will know
when their minds are going astray. Then it is time to obtain profes-
sional medical help, and the church leaders should form groups for
assistance.

Numerous states have decided to address mental health issues—
children and adults who have mental issues—and buy guns. Now
one of the problems is that it is hard to get the church's support for
such an effort because of the lobbyists. In dealing with gun issues, the

lobbyists believe that you should leave those things alone. Whereas as Christians, we should consider the falling.

Actions

What is God's people's primary source of service?

> Thy word is a lamp unto my feet, and a light unto my path. I Have sworn, and I will perform it, that I will keep thy righteous judgment. I am afflicted very much: quicken me, O Lord, according unto word. Accept, I beseech thee, the freewill offering of my mouth, O Lord, and teach me thy judgments. (Psalm 119:105–108)

And church leaders work with the lobbyists! The problems occurring in our lives are occurring by reason of "truth" or "falsehood." The truth is Jesus the Lord, and Satan the devil is falsehood as set forth herein (devil mind-binding spirit).

True or false:

> Ye cannot serve God and mammon. (Luke 16:12)

In the last few days, several killings and injuries have occurred in Dayton, Ohio's mass shooting. Furthermore, there are twenty dead and twenty-six injured in the El Paso mass shooting.

We can be sure, with these things occurring, that the devil is dealing with the spirit of our minds. The Lord has prophesied in the last few days.

> No servant can serve two masters: for either he will hate the one and love the other; or else he will hold to one and despise the other. Ye cannot serve God and mammon. (Luke 16:13)

Comply with the Truth

In fact, the most valuable lesson humanity has learned from philosophy is that it is impossible to make sense of truth without acknowledging God as a necessary starting point.

I believe that God has a plan for me in the prophecy. Talking to people, I understand their main thoughts right now.

1. Many do not care about going to hell. They give no thought to what results this world will require of them. They don't think. They are doing exactly what the devil requires them to do. In most cases, they are in an organization, which is pushing them and planning their ways.
2. In some cases, those people do not have a sound mind, and when a person with a bad mind becomes exposed to hate, the devil hastily takes them into destruction (produces bitter fruit).

Where Will You Spend Eternity?

a. A lot of people do not care about eternity.
b. Some families do not teach their children about Jesus.
c. In the past, people hung and burned people with children watching (producing hate and bitter fruit).
d. Today, people are going into the street, clubs, etc., looking to murder as many as possible.
e. They are backing and supporting hate organizations, seeking to kill as many as possible.

THOSE ORGANIZATIONS PUSH PEOPLE AND TEACH HATING AND KILLING, PRODUCING BITTER ROOTS AND FRUIT. When you have no concern about the results of your action, you, as Christians, have lost it all.

We have not stood fast in our effort to preach and teach Jesus, love, and truth because we failed to take a stand against injustice. The problem now is for those people who do not teach the youth the error of such thinking. The youth then go off and commit such killings, such as those that just occurred.

It's now time for the church leaders to come forth, see the present circumstances, and explain to their church members that there are some errors that need to be addressed, including the allowance of misrepresentation to allow their children to believe that they are special by being White, and explain that they must also come to Jesus and walk as the word has set forth.

God has stated that he is unhappy with us. Sin is committed. The problem is our failure to address sin.

> Woe be unto the pastors that destroy and scatter the sheep of my pasture! Sith the LORD. Therefore thus saith the Lord God of Israel against the pastors that feed my people; Ye have scattered my flock, and driven them away, and have not visited them: behold I will visit upon you the evil of your doing, saith the Lord. And I will gather the remnant of my flock out of all countries whither I have driven and will bring them again to their folds; and they shall be fruitful and increase. (Jeremiah 23:1–5)

In judgment, the righteous shall be justified, and the unjust shall be punished. We must understand that a stand for righteousness must be taken.

God sees us for who we are. John the Baptist lost his life for speaking about righteousness (Mark 6:14–29). We must stand against unrighteousness.

The church does not oppose the business issues the gun lobbyists are supporting. And we know that's wrong. Our motive for any effort or action should never serve negative or ungodly purposes, which could deter people from committing to Christ or accepting the gospel.

AND MY POSITION ON MILITARY WEAPONS IS THAT THEY SHOULD NOT BE ALLOWED FOR USE

ON OUR STREETS, KILLING OUR CHILDREN AND TEACHERS AT SCHOOLS, MURDERING PEOPLE IN OUR SYNAGOGUES, CHURCHES, CLUBS, ETC. As a Christian, do not just keep quiet; fulfill your responsibility to righteousness and stand for righteousness. Just as John the Baptist stood against injustice (which he died for), so should we!

> And I will set up shepherds over them which shall feed them: and they shall fear no more, nor be dismayed, neither shall be lacking, say the Lord. (Jeremiah 23:4 KJV)

Of course, God's own motives, purposes, and actions are emphatically pure and holy all the time (Genesis 50:20). He accomplishes good in and through all things, and that includes all the evil done by the power of darkness.

The will to sin is always from the sinner's own heart, not from God. He is never the author or cause of evil.

It is time the church leaders, as well as family members, stop and look at the damage past offenses are imposing on the youth. You can correct a problem once you realize that it is a problem, which is the reason for this part of this book. THIS WILL SERVE TWO PURPOSES: STOP THE KILLING AND PROVIDE SALVATION FOR THE LOST SOULS BECAUSE THERE IS NO REPENTANCE ONCE THE "FLYING ROLL" GOES FORTH.

Furthermore, notice that both the false prophet and the people who departed from God's word to follow their lying words will all suffer God's judgment. But the multiple warnings are also reminders to all faithful about this seriousness of the truth, which is urging us to rise and content earnestly for the faith against the devil and their false teaching.

> Lying lips are an abomination to the Lord [which is DONALD TRUMP], but those who act faithfully are his delight. (Proverbs 12:22)

THOSE MISLEADING PASTORS NEED TO REPENT. AS MEN AND WOMEN OF GOD, WE MUST COMMIT OURSELVES TO A FAITHFUL STAND ON TRUTH. DECISIONS SHOULD BE MADE WITH FEAR AND TREMBLING. When seeing the answers (we should pray and wait to hear from the Holy Ghost), "we must take a stance for righteousness." John the Baptist lost his life for standing up for righteousness (Mark 6:14–29).

Stand for Truth

It's in such areas as this that I mention *Battlefield of the Mind*. I read the book, and if you had also, you would be in a better position mentally to deal with this situation. A double-minded man is unstable in all his ways. God's plan is taking a step. I look at unbelievers, people who do not know God, do not want to know Him, and say that they do not need Him, and I wonder how they can have that kind of belief. They appear to not have an awareness of something lacking in their lives. They seem to be totally happy doing those things. That, to me, is meaningless without God.

No matter what you went through in the past, how many setbacks you've suffered, or who or what has tried to hinder your progress, today is another day, and the Lord wants to do a new thing in your life. Do not let your past determine your future.

But the fact is that my fifty years of studying the Bible and prophecy keep me motivated to fulfill my commission to the Lord— go into the highways and byways and restrain men from coming. I feel pressed to reach mankind and know that the effort I'm putting forth won't be in vain because I'm constantly looking to reach mankind by the will of God. They seem to have walked away from God.

I cannot determine if COVID-19 has anything to do with the prophecy, but I can see where it has brought man's attention to Jesus. I truly believe that with all of God's people in this nation, there are enough believers once this book, *The Flying Roll*, goes forth to open the minds of men to consider the bad circumstances that have occurred.

Furthermore, on August 26, 2020, on the news, Donald Trump stated that Jerry Falwell Jr. had a lot to do with his election win in 2016, helping him with the church. Since Christians supported Trump in 2016, we have seen an almost complete term for his actions and the people he called friends:

1. Jerry Falwell Jr. is now seeing the Christian choices he has made. We look at the activities that Trump has done, which have been set forth in this book.
2. He started by cheating on his family. His sister set forth claims, which have been set forth in paperwork. Trump lies and manipulates in dividing his father's estate. He gave little to the family and improperly kept most of the estate.
3. Moving on to his business activities, he set up a business, ensuring people that he would teach them how to be millionaires.
4. He was sued for that and had to pay a $25 million settlement.
5. Moving on to other businesses, he built hotels. When the work on the hotels was complete, Trump refused to pay the contractors. A few contractors collected their money; the majority have remaining debts owed.
6. A Senate report shows that in 2016, the Trump campaign worked with Russian intelligence. And we can see that President Trump never speaks against Putin or Russia about anything.
7. Our intelligence report says that Russia paid for the killing of American soldiers during the war. The president accepts Putin's word, who said that they did not do that.
8. Trump ordered to pay $44,100 in attorney fees to porn actress Stormy Daniels to pay for her legal battle over her effort to cancel a hush money deal broker to keep her quiet about their sexual relationship. (When Trump has 35 percent followers who say he never lies.) Those believers (35 percent of whom) are Christians.

AND BY THE GRACE OF GOD, BEGIN TO APPLY CHRISTIAN PRINCIPLES OF LOVE TO THE CIRCUMSTANCES IN OUR COUNTRY AND TURN AGAINST AND AWAY FROM HATE. It's now time for the church leaders to come and set forth the present circumstances and explain to their church members that there are some errors that need to be addressed. There is no allowance for misrepresentation when parents allow their children to believe they are special by being White and explain that they must also come to Jesus and walk with faith and love.

We are the United States of America; by that, I mean that our money reads, "In God we trust." We have taken a stance before the world, "We stand for Christ." NOW WE ARE LETTING OTHERS STEP FORTH WITH MESSAGES TO REDEFINE US AS TO WHAT WE STAND FOR.

Consider Donald Trump (12/20/2021). He is no longer the president, but we must still consider his actions. Prior to January 6, he went on the media and asked his followers to come to the Washington Capitol Building to defend him and demand their rights to this country because they will not receive their rights through weakness; they must fight for them.

And as Christians, we are backed off to a corner and refuse to speak for righteousness, while a White supremist group now represents us. The White supremist should look at the past before God destroyed the first world.

Let's look at some of the people in that world. Goliath is nine feet and six inches tall because, in that world, demonic men joined with women to have children—Goliath being a result. WILL THE POWER BE MIGHTY? WHILE KILLING PEOPLE WITHOUT CAUSE, WILL THAT MAKE YOU SOMETHING TODAY? IN THE PAST, IT DIDN'T MAKE GOLIATH ANYTHING. God has promised that he is going to send forth "the flying roll" across the face of this world, which will bring a curse upon the ungodly.

And looking at COVID-19, we don't have a clear understanding of what the full effect of it will be or how far it will go. Today, there are great dangers facing the church, including apathy toward the truth and indifference about false teachings. Truthfully, we are not particularly good these days at guarding the truth.

Look at the fact that approximately forty-two million people voted for President Trump, and some of his followers are members of a cult called Q. We are living in a world where cameras are everywhere, with newscasts continuously recording numerous conversations. We have some people who are caught on film making statements and then say, "I did not make that statement." They want you to accept their double statements as facts. That's President Trump.

We Are the Lying Generation

When the facts above exist, we are then living under the influence of the devil because he is the father of lies. You are not on the fence anymore, and Christian people should pay attention. As a matter of fact, the scripture says that those who are merely combative, aggressive, or quarrelsome are unfit for spiritual leadership. In 1 Timothy 3:3, "When Paul laid out the qualification for church leaders, he does so fairly and clearly, a servant of the Lord must not quarrel but be gentle to all."

As men and women of God, we are to examine ourselves because we cannot attach ourselves to and be followers of those who are not in keeping with the will of God and truth.

Back to Prophecy

Picture B7a. The British Commonwealth Occupation Force (BCOF) is also one of the four ruling heads of Japan. The BCOF was the name of the joint Australian, British Indian Army, and New Zealand military force in occupied Japan from February 21, 1946, until the end of the occupation in 1952.

Picture D: The chart from the fall of the Roman kingdom to the establishment of Christ's kingdom. This chart sets forth the three comings of Christ. This prophecy is not given in 1-2-3 or A-B-C order; therefore, this document must be introduced at this time, which seems to be out of order. Now coming two and three below, are at different times. In "The Marriage Supper of the Lamb," Jesus is the bridegroom. The other two "comings" are at a later time.

Now we must set forth the illustrations and the following kingdoms, which are the governments mentioned below.

Picture B1: Julius Caesar, the first king. The rise of Rome to world power under Julius Caesar, the kingship of Rome, started with Julius Caesar and ended with Theodosius II, AD 450, when the great horn was broken.

Picture B2: History of Anglo-Saxon England. As the Roman occupation of Britain was ending, Constantine III withdrew the remains of the army in reaction to the barbarians' invasion of Europe. The Romano-British leaders were faced with an increasing security problem from the seaborne raids, particularly by Picts on the east coast of England. The expedient adopted by the Romano-British leaders was to entitle them to the help of Anglo-Saxon mercenaries (known as foederati), to whom they ceded territory. In about AD 442, the Anglo-Saxons mutinied, apparently because they had not been paid. The British responded by appealing to the Roman commander of the Western empire, Aetius, for help (a document known as the Groans of the Britons), even though the Western Roman Emperor had written to the British civitas in or about AD 410, telling them to look to their own defense. There then followed several years of fighting between the British and the Anglo-Saxons. The fighting continued until about AD 500.

PICTURE B3: THIS DOCUMENT ILLUSTRATES INFORMATION THAT SETS FORTH THE RISE OF ENGLAND AS A WORLD POWER. Theodosius settled the military situation in the east through a four-year war against the Goths, ending in a peace treaty in 382. This set a dubious precedent by allowing the Visigoths to settle on lands within the empire under the authority of their own king rather than any imperial official.

Picture B4: England, the first nation to rise to world power after Alexander's death. King Alexander died in 323 BC, which is before the birth of Christ, and history does not show any world nation extending from that point in time until today. England became a world power in 382 BC.

Picture B5: United States of America. At the Second Continental Congress, after the thirteen colonies voted to declare independence from Great Britain, the colonies determined that they needed an official seal. So Dr. Franklin, Mr. J. Adams, and Mr. Jefferson, as a committee, prepared a device for a seal of the United States of America. However, the only portion of the design accepted by the Congress was the statement *E pluribus unum.* Six years and two committees later, in May 1782, the brother of a Philadelphian naturalist provided a drawing showing an eagle displayed as the symbol of "supreme power and authority." Congress liked the drawing, so before the end of 1782, an eagle holding a bundle of arrows in one talon and an olive branch in the other was accepted as the seal.

Picture B6: Soviet Union. This shows the history of Soviet Russia and the Soviet Union (1917–1927), from the October Revolution to the Stains consolidation of power.

Picture B7: Japan is the leopard. In Revelations 13:2, "After this I beheld, and lo another, like a leopard, which had upon the back of it four wings of a foul; the beast had also four heads; and dominion was given to it."

The leopard must rise to power after the rise of the bear "Russia" in 1922.

> The first was like a lion and had eagle's wing: I beheld till the wings thereof were plucked, and it was lifted from the earth, and made to stand upon the feet as a man, and a man's heart was given to it. And behold another beast, a second, like to a bear and it raised up itself on one side, and it had three ribs in the mouth of it between the teeth of it: and they said thus unto it, Arise, devour mush flesh. After this I beheld, and lo another, like a leopard, which had upon the back of it four

wings of a fowl; the beast had also four heads; and dominion was given to it. (Daniel 7:4–6)

The leopard is the symbolic animal for Japan. It is considered to be lucky. Another one, like a leopard, had on its back the four wings of a fowl; the beast also had four heads, and dominion was given to it.

1. Lion for the sinners—this second part will come later in the prophecy.
2. Judgment day upon the earth

THE COMING OF CHRIST IS ALSO SET FORTH IN THE FOLLOWING DOCUMENT.

Picture E of the document below has the same image but different names. Furthermore, different information is set forth in my "teaching outline" under number vi.

1. The stone was cut out without hands, showing the picture where the kingdom of God struck the feet of the Colossus.
2. Furthermore, the coming of the kingdom of Christ, striking the beast, are also the feet.

The bottom of the picture shows the kingdom of God striking the one-world government, "the beast." God foretold in picture b, 2,500 years ago, that Jesus's coming kingdom would destroy the world kingdoms of today. And because it was stated for all world governments, we see that this is the point—to set forth the illustrations of all governments.

Because this is prophecy: The one-world government is also displayed as picture b, "the beast with seven heads." "Beast" is defined on the content sheet in this book as a "**government**" or political power." So now we know that the kingdom of God is hitting and destroying a "government," which is below. The names of the governments are as follows:

a. England
b. USA
c. USSR
d. Japan and China

Government is what these four nations are—a government.

Note:

> They shall mingle themselves with the seeds of
> men: but they shall not cleave one to another.
> And in the days of those kings shall the God of
> heaven set up a kingdom. Which shall never be
> destroyed. (Daniel 2:43–44)

THE SCRIPTURE ABOVE MENTIONS DEMONIC BEINGS MINGLING THEMSELVES WITH THE SEED OF MEN. NOW THAT IS A SITUATION THAT OCCURS IN THE ONE-WORLD GOVERNMENT.

Picture Ea: The one-world government.
Time of the Fourth Great Kingdom

1. England, AD 449,   Caesar
Lion with eagle wings
2. USA, 1776
3. USSR, 1917, Bear   Generals
4. a. Japan, 1988, Leopard   Senate
b. China, 666, Devil   Dragon

Picture Eb: One-world government, "The Rise of the Antichrist."
The fourth kingdom "defines the fourth beast."

Picture Eb1. The fourth beast will be the last four world powers
upon the earth, which will be formed into a one-world government
(the beast) (Daniel 7:3, 4, 5, 6).

Once again, those four beasts have been mentioned, again and again, we must refer back now to picture j, for definition; (the beast is also defined as a "kingdom") and that is what we must now go forth with.

THE KINGDOMS WE ARE NOW MAKING REFERENCE TO ARE THE SAID KINGDOMS OF TODAY.

1. England
2. USA
3. USSR
4. a. Japan
   b. China

These great beasts, which are four, are four kings, which shall rise out of the earth. (Daniel 7:17)

1. And four great beasts came up from the sea, diverse one from another.
2. The first was like a lion and had eagle wings: I beheld till the wings thereof were plucked, and it was lifted from the earth and made stand upon the feet as a man, and a man's heart was given to it.
3. And behold another beast, a second, like a bear, and it raised itself on one side, and it had three ribs in the mouth of it between the teeth of it; and they said thus unto it, Arise, devour much flesh.
4. After this, I beheld, and lo, another, like a leopard, which had on the back of it the four wings of a fowl; the beast also had four heads; and dominion was given to it.

We must now refer to *image* 24, which shows the picture of the leopard being mentioned above, showing "the four ruling heads of Japan."

1. The name of the leopard is "the Senate, meaning the body." It's called the body because that is the portion of it in the one-world government.
2. THIS IS THE PART OF THE BOOK WHERE IMAGE 24 IS MANIFESTED: "Sit forth" (the beast) now to set forth the beast.
3. "Leopard," the beast, is illustrated as follows: the four nations of today—England, the USA, the USSR, Japan, and China.

And the beast which I saw was like unto a leopard, and his feet were as the feet of a bear, and his mouth as the mouth of a lion: and the dragon gave him his power and his seat, and great authority. (Revelations 13:2)

The Lord's interpretation of today's nations is that "they are beasts." Therefore, we set them forth as follows:

1. England's represented beast is a "lion" with "eagle wings" (the head of the leopard).
2. USSR "Soviet Union" (feet of the leopard)—"law enforcement body of the government"
3. a. Japan (body of the leopard)—"Senate"
   b. China

THE FACT IS THAT THE SAINTS TAKE THE KINGDOM FROM THOSE FOUR, WHICH IS IN FACT PROOF THAT THOSE ARE THE LAST KINGDOMS OF MAN.

Picture E2: One-world government—the fourth kingdom. After the rise of the one-world government, the Antichrist shall come to power. The feet of the Colossus is the fourth kingdom (the rise of the Antichrist).

Thus he said, forth beast shall be the fourth kingdom upon the earth, which shall be diverse from all kingdoms, and shall devour the hole earth, and shall tread it down, and break it in pieces. (Daniel 7:23)

Refer to *picture Ea.*

And the ten horns out of this kingdom are ten kings that shall arise: and another shall rise after them; and he shall be diverse from the first, and he shall subdue three kings. (Daniel 7:24)

For more insight, we're referring to *picture E2* as follows:

And I saw one of his heads as it were wounded to death; and his deadly wound was healed. (Revelation 13:3)

The Wounded Head of the Beast Is Healed Explained

The ten kings are referred to as ten governors.

And the ten horns which thou saw are ten kings, which have received no kingdom yet; but receive power as kings one hour with the beast. (Revelation 17:12)

The governors are granted power in the one-world government. THE STRUCTURE OF THIS GOVERNMENT IS THE SAME AS THE ROMAN ORDER OF GOVERNMENT:

a. England is represented by a beast as a "lion" with "eagle wings" (which is the head).
b. USSR "Soviet Union" (feet of the leopard)
c. 1. Japan (body of the leopard)
2. China. (All shown in *picture Ea*)

In essence, this is what God calls the "wounded head of the beast"—a renewed Roman order of government for today (the one-world government).

> And he shall speak great words against the most High and shall wear out the saints of the most High and think to change times and laws: and they shall be given into his hands until a time and times and the dividing of time. But the judgement shall sit, and they shall take away his dominion, to consume and to destroy it until the end. And the kingdom and dominion, and the greatness of the kingdom under the whole heaven, shall be given to the people of the saints of the Highest, whose kingdom is an everlasting kingdom, and all dominions shall serve and obey him. (Daniel 7:25–27)

Picture F: Time of the kingdom of the Antichrist—the fourth kingdom. It is labeled with scriptures of the Antichrist's actions. His actions are listed thereon the picture, as follows. (You must examine *picture F* while doing the study.)

1. He rules over the Roman Empire (the beast).
2. He will rise and become STRONG with small PEOPLE.
3. He will rise as a vile person, from the people.
4. He shall kill the saints and cause fire to come down from heaven. Craft shall prosper in his hand.
5. He shall cause man to receive the MARK of the BEAST.
6. He shall confirm the COVENT with many for one week.

Picture G: The time of the kingdom of Christ.

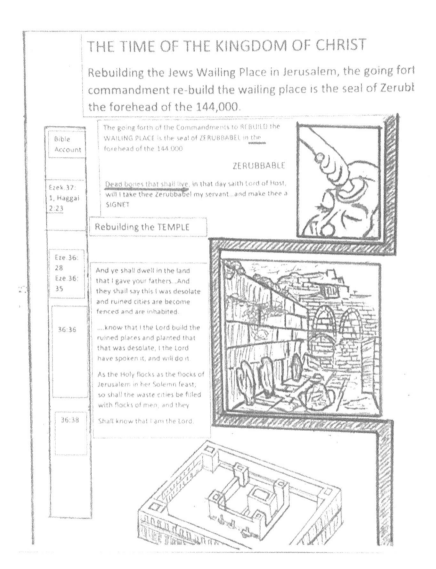

THE TIME OF THE KINGDOM OF CHRIST

Rebuilding the Jews Wailing Place in Jerusalem, the going fort
commandment re-build the wailing place is the seal of Zerubb
the forehead of the 144,000.

Bible Account	The going forth of the Commandments to REBUILD the WAILING PLACE is the seal of ZERUBBABEL in the forehead of the 144,000
	ZERUBBABLE
Ezek 37: 1, Haggai 2.23	Dead bones that shall live, in that day saith Lord of Host, will I take thee Zerubbabel my servant...and make thee a SIGNET
	Rebuilding the TEMPLE
Eze 36: 28 Eze 36: 35	And ye shall dwell in the land that I gave your fathers...And they shall say this I was desolate and ruined cities are become fenced and are inhabited.
36:36	...know that I the Lord build the ruined places and planted that that was desolate, I the Lord have spoken it, and will do it
	As the Holy flocks as the flocks of Jerusalem in her Solemn feast; so shall the waste cities be filled with flocks of men; and they
36:38	Shall know that I am the Lord.

The Sealing of the 144,000

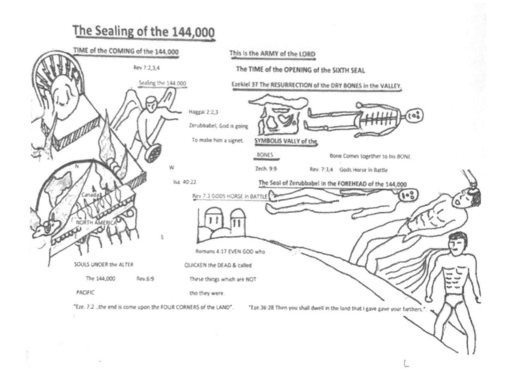

TIME of the COMING of the 144,000

Rev 7:2,3,4

Sealing the 144,000

This is the ARMY of the LORD

The TIME of the OPENING of the SIXTH SEAL

Ezekiel 37 The RESURRECTION of the DRY BONES in the VALLEY

Haggai 2:2,3

Zerubbabel, God is going

To make him a signet.

SYMBOLIS VALLEY of the

BONES

Bone Comes together to his BONE

Zech. 9:9   Rev. 7:3,4   Gods Horse in Battle

Isa. 40:22

The Seal of Zerubbabel in the FOREHEAD of the 144,000

Canada

Rev. 7:3 GODS HORSE in BATTLE

N

NORTH AMERICA

W

S

Romans 4:17 EVEN GOD who

SOULS UNDER the ALTER

QUICKEN the DEAD & called

The 144,000   Rev.6:9

These things which are NOT

PACIFIC

tho they were.

"Eze. 7:2 ..the end is come upon the FOUR CORNERS of the LAND".   "Eze. 36:28 Then you shall dwell in the land that I gave gave your farthers.".

The Sealing of the 144,000

All the things in this book must be from Scripture.

And after these things I saw four angles standing on the four corners of the earth, holding the four winds of the earth, that the wind should not blow on the earth, nor on any tree. And I saw another angel ascending from the east, having the seal of the living God: and he cried with a loud voice to the four angels, to whom it is given to hurt the earth and the sea, saying, hurt not the earth, neither the sea, nor the trees, till we have sealed the servants of our God in their foreheads. And I heard the number of them which were sealed: and there were sealed a hundred and forty and four thousand of all the tribes of the children of Israel. (Revelation 7:1–4)

The fact is that God told the four angels who were going to hurt the earth to stop until he had sealed his 144,000 in their forehead. (Those issues are set forth in *picture G.*) Furthermore, He said that He was going to rebuild the temple. To illustrate the action of the 144,000, we set forth the picture as follows: (You must view this picture while studying.) The end has come.

> Also, thou son of man, thus say the Lord God unto the land of Israel, an end, the end is come upon the four corners of the land. (Ezekiel 7:2)

> An end is come, the end is come: it watches for thee; behold, it is come. (Ezekiel 7:6)

> Now will I shortly pour out my fury upon thee and accomplish mine anger upon thee: and I will judge thee according to thy ways, and will recompense thee for all thine, abominations. (Ezekiel 7:8)

Picture Ha. After Jesus takes his people in the catching away (Rapture), the things shall come upon the earth thereafter.

Picture Hb. The sun shall be turned into darkness and the moon into blood before the great and terrible day of the Lord comes.

Picture I: The time of the opening of the six seals. It shows the second coming of Christ, Ezekiel's cherubim (the four angels), "the four seals," and the time of the opening of the six seals.

> For there shall be great tribulation such as was since the beginning, of the world to this time, nor ever shall be. (Matthews 24:21)

> A fire devoured before them, and behind them a flame burriest; the land is as the garden of Eden

before them, and behind them a desolate wild-
ness; yea and nothing shall escape them. (Joel 2:3)

In Conclusion

THIS STUDY IS DESIGN TO SERVE ONLY ONE PURPOSE
THAT IS TO PROVE GOD'S WORD IS ALL TRUE, 2500 YEARS
GOD NAMED EVERY WORLD KINGDOM THAT WOULD RISE
INCLUDING THE KINGDOM OF THE ANTICHRIST AND THE
COMING KINGDON OF CHRIST

Fact: Better than 90% of the Book of Revelations is now History!
Question: Who is there that do not understand History?

Revelations was written approximately
1914 years ago, and was interrupted
by Daniel approximately 2500
years ago. I set forth 10 years
of research, which I finished
in 1988, explaining 90%
of Revelations is
Now History

IS THIS
REALY THE WAY

Prior to attending you need to look up,

Definition of Revelation (Words) Literal Meaning

1. **Head:** Major Power, Rulers, Government:
Defined in; Daniel 7:6, Daniel 8:8 though 22, Daniel 18:18 and Relation 17:3 though 10.

2. **Beast:** Kingdom, Government, Political Power.
Defined in; Daniel 7:23.

3. **Horn;** Power and Strength, King or Kingdom.
Defined in; Deuteronomy 33:17, Zechariah 1:1:18. Psalms 89:17 though 24 and Daniel 8:5 though 21,22.

TODAY WE ARE LIVING THE CURRENT EVENTS
OF GOD'S (PROPHECY)

Isaiah 46:9,10
GOD SAID ONLY HE CAN DECLARE WHAT THE ENDING WILL BE AT BEGINNING
AND THAT HIS COUNSEL SHALL STAND, AND HE WILL DO HIS PLEASURE

DO NOT WAIT UNTIL IT'S TO LATE, TO UNDERSTAND THE SIGNS
OF THE TIMES.

BIBICAL WORDS DIFINITIONS

It require a proper understanding of the biblical words, to understand revelations. The symbols below are used.

1. **Beast,** Kingdom, government, political power. Daniel 7:23.
2. **Wild Beast out of the sea,** a Political Power and a person, revelations 13: 1-10.
3. **Wild Beast,** revelation 13:1,2
4. **Heads,** Major powers, rulers governments, Daniel 7:6, Daniel 8:8, 22, revelations 17,3,10.
5. **Horn,** Power and strength, Deuteronomy 33:17, Zechariah 1:18,19.
6. **Lambs wife,** New Jerusalem, Revelation 19:7-9, 21:2,9,10.
7. **Mountains,** Political or religio/political powers, Isaiah 2:2,3 Jeremiah 17:3 , 31:23, Jeremiah 51:24,25.
8. **Mountain,** Jeremiah 51:25, 25 Behold I am against thee, O destroying mountain, saith the Lord, which destroyest all the earth: and I will stretch out mine hand upon thee and roll the down from the rocks and will make thee a burnt mountain.
9. **Isaiah 2:1, 1.** The word that Isaiah the son of Amoz saw concerning Judah and Jerusalem.
10. **2.** And it shall come to pass in the last days, that the **mountain of the Lord's house** shall be established in the **top** of the **mountains** and shall **be exalted above the hills;** and all nations shall flow unto it.
11. **Mountains,** Political or religio/political powers, Isaiah 2:2,3 Jeremiah 17:3 , 31:23, Jeremiah 51:24,25.
12. **Man child,** Jesus, Psalms 2:7-9, Revelations 12: 5.
13. **Second Death,** Lake of fire, Revelation 21:8 , 20:14.
14. **Seven Lamps,** Jesus, Word of God. Symbol of harvest-End of world, Matthew 13:39, Revelation 14:14.
15. **Red (color),** Sin corruption. Isaiah 1:18, 26:21, Psalm 75:8, Jeremiah 46:10.
16. **Sickle** Symbol of harvest – End of the world, Matthew 13:9, Revelations 14:14.

17. **Winds** Strife, commotion, "winds of war" Jeremiah 25:31-33-49:36,36, Zechariah 7;14.
18. **Wrath of God**   Seven last plagues   Revelations 15:1.
19. **Woman, Pure**   Apostate Church~ Jeremiah 6:2, Isaiah 51:16, Ephesians 5:22-35.
20. **Seven Heads** Seven political powers~. Revelations 17:9, Isaiah 2:2-4, Jeremiah 17:3.

COPY EXPLAINING PROPHECY

THE PROPHECY OF GOD IS PROVEN TRUE BY WORLD HISTORY

2500 Years ago, the prophet Daniel explained the world kingdoms, from the first world kingdom of King Nebuchadnezzar, to the coming kingdom of Christ.

NOTE THAT HEREON IS BOTH WORLD HISTORY, COMPARED TO PROPHECY.

Bible Account	PROPHECY	B.C. Approx	HISTORY
Dan 2:31	Daniel Interpreted	602	Daniel was taken to Babylon in 605 B.C.
44	Nebuchadnezzar Dream		Daniel was included the death sentence.
			History show King Belshazzar's Kingdom
Dan 2:31	Daniel Numbered		Fell to the kings of Media and Persia the
	Every coming Kingdom	602	Ram, Dream explained it 11 years prior
	Prophecy of the Ram and	536	Babylon fell 536 B.C.
Dan 8:3	Prophecy of the Goat.		
			History shows King Belshazzar's Kingdom Fell to the
			Kings of Media and Persia Ram
			BABYLON FELL 536 B.C.
Dan 8:3	The Prophecy of the GOAT	550	
			History Show Persia Fell to as Daniel Prophesied
			220 years prior
Daniel's Interpretation of		330	Year of the fall of Persia
	Of the king of Greece		History shows the king to rise up at the Fall of
Dan 8:20	THE PROPHECY		GREECE was the king of ROME prophecy 345
	Of the great horn of the		
	He GOAT being broken		years prior the brake up of GREECE.
	And FOUR HORNS		History shows that at the fall of ROME FOUR

NATIONS came to world power and are yet world powers.

ENGLAND U.S.A. U.S.S.R. CHINA/JAPAN

603 The Lord Gave King Nebuchadnezzar the Name of All
WORLD KINGDOMS

The Prophecy of God is Proven True By WORLD

HISTORY

THAT 2500 YEARS AGO, the PROPHET DANIEL NAMED
every WORKD KINGDOM, from the FIRST WORLD
KINGDOM of NEBUCHADNEZZAR until the COMING of
the KINGDOM of CHRIST.

NOTE: Below is BOTH WORLD HISTORY as COMPARED
to PROPHECY

| B.C. |

Bible Account | DANIEL INTERPET NEBUCHADNEZZAR DREAM-Daniel 22:1-5

| APPROX |

| TIME |

PROPHECY		HISTORY
Dan. 2:31	Daniel Interpret Nebuchadnezzar Dream	602	Daniel was taken to Babylon by King Nebuchadnezzar in 605
Though 44 death sentence by Nebuchadnezzar, Relating to King Nebuchadnezzar's Dream.			B.C., Daniel and his companions were included under the
	from 1988		
Dan. 2:31 though 44	DANIEL NUMBERED EVERY UNTIL THE COMING OFR THE	602	WORLD KINGDOM THAT WOULD RISE AND FALL KINGDOM OF CHRIST

The Prophecy of the RAM | from 1988 | History shows KING BELSHAZZAR'S

Dan. 8:3   Daniel had the Prophecy of | 550 | KINGDOM FELL to the KINGS of

though 26 | the RAM and the GOAT | | MEDIA and PERSIA . "the RAM"

The HORNS of the RAM | | Daniels Dream of the RAM foretold
Are the Kings of Media | | the FALL of BABYON

And PERSIA | 536 | BABYON FELL 536 B.C.

Dan. 8:3   The PROPHECY of the | 550

WE ARE IN THE LAST GENERATION.

1. There is no ministry today addressing a message to today's generation.
2. There are a lot of ministries that address their messages around the Old Testament.
3. Issues revolve around the Old Testament.
4. Issues accrue around the church at those times.

ONE THING THAT IS DIFFERENT ABOUT THIS GENERATION IS THAT THERE ARE LARGE MINIS-TRIES WRITING THEIR OWN BIBLES. The problem I have with that is that, in reading some of those Bibles, there are some word changes, in relation to the "King James Bible," and those word changes mean a different meaning.

So because of the problems occurring in this generation, we must address the issues occurring in this generation. In our attempt to address today's issues, we must also address the problems attached to the issues of today, such as

1. COVID-19 and
2. confronting a lying generation.

In thinking it through, I am considering this: I did not know how to start a book or end one. I know that I read evangelist Joyce Meyer's book, *Battlefield of the Mind*, further. Because Joyce Meyer carefully and elaborately details the issues of the mind while reading, I can see that people living in this generation of lies can benefit from reading and understanding the book. This is why we are recommending to those who don't have the book that they buy one, and that would make it much easier to understand our book **and keep a mind set on the truth.**

Winning people to Christ depends on the conditions you are dealing with.

I. **At the Time of Goliath**
   1. Being a big, strong warrior was enough. Goliath was nine feet and six inches tall, a warrior big enough to kill and destroy.
   2. The power of the world was being big and strong enough to kill and destroy.

II. **The God-King**
   1. The Egyptians first based their authority on Egyptian religious beliefs. The Egyptians believed that God controlled everything that happened on earth.
   2. Because the pharaoh controlled Egypt, people naturally saw him or her as the god-king.
   3. The most powerful person in ancient Egypt was the pharaoh, which made him the religious leader of the Egyptian people as well.

III. **Religious Leaders and the President**
   1. IN THE UNITED STATES, WE HAVE OUR RELIGIOUS LEADERS AND A PRESIDENT, WHICH IS SIMILAR TO EGYPT. They had a pharaoh, who was also their religious leader.

NOW THE POINT I AM TRYING TO MAKE IS THIS:

   2. The religious leader and the pharaoh were one. Back then, they did not separate government leadership from religious leadership.

IN CONTINUATION OF THAT POINT:

   3. We are forced today to address President Trump and his relationship with religion.

IV. **Agreement with Church Leaders**

    1. IN OUR COUNTRY, PRESIDENT TRUMP HAS CONCLUDED AN AGREEMENT WITH THE CHURCH LEADERS OF TODAY. IN THE MEDIA, HE TOLD THEM THAT HE HAD GIVEN US EVERYTHING WE ASKED OF HIM. SO WHAT ARE WE COMPLAINING ABOUT NOW?

    2. PRESIDENT TRUMP CONFIRMS IN HIS STATEMENTS WHAT HE SAID IN THE PAST: THAT JERRY FALWELL JR. HELPED HIM REACH AN AGREEMENT WITH THE CHURCH LEADERS IN 2016 FOR THEIR SUPPORT.

The fact is that the Lord wants us to follow Him and not make deals with lying and corrupt politicians. Now the religious leaders have a conditional agreement with the president. THEY ARE NOT WORRIED ABOUT THEIR AGREEMENT WITH THE GOSPEL. But as Christians, what is the most important thing we seek to accomplish down here?

Actions

WHAT IS GOD'S PEOPLE PRIMARY SOURCE OF SERVICE TO THIS WORLD?

> Thy word is a lamp unto my feet, and a light unto my path. I Have sworn, and I will perform it, that I will keep thy righteous judgment. (Psalm 119:105–106)

INSTEAD OF FOLLOWING THE WILL AND WORD OF GOD, THEY ARE FOLLOWING THEIR COMMITMENT TO PRESIDENT TRUMP. Speaking of Christian leadership, they not only had an agreement with President

Trump, but through Trump, they have agreed to ignore and support the rifle association.

All their different agreements put us in a position where we are forced to challenge them because they have ignored the following:

1. **God's People's Primary Source of Service to This World**

    We are living in the last generation. There is no comparison between this generation and others. In this generation, there are people who attend school and are educated in manipulation.

2. **THE IMPOSSIBILITY OF CONNECTING LIES AND FACTS**

    Because Joyce Meyers carefully and elaborately details the issues of the mind while reading, I can see that people living in this generation of lies can benefit from reading and understanding the book. Therefore, we recommend the purchase of *Battlefield of the Mind* to those who don't have one.

    Because politics plays an especially significant role in our lives today, all aspects of our lives are involved in politics. That is in part because of COVID-19, which is a worldwide problem.

    We are forced by circumstances to confront numerous issues in world events because President Trump is such a ridiculous liar and will confront and fight you if you do not agree with his lies.

3. **Misleading Leadership**

    AND WE CANNOT AGREE WITH TRUMP BECAUSE OF HIS AGREEMENT WITH THE CHRISTIAN COMMUNITY. Through that agreement, the Christian followers are being misled by his leadership.

    We can only win fellowship with the Lord through his word and truth. Our nation is torn with prejudice, which is increased by White supremist actions.

    We feel a sense of responsibility toward our Christian brothers and sisters. Our enemy is Satan, and he has a strong hold on society. The enemies who are speaking forth this day are haters, such as the White Nationalists.

There are some White groups that say their race is their religion. As they go forth hating and killing, fully conforming to our claim, their choice of hate is more important to them than their fear of hell. Satan is in control of that society.

4. **Appeal to Christian Community Leaders**

THERE ARE ONLY A FEW PEOPLE TODAY WHO HAVE THE AUTHORITY TO GO FORTH AS CHRISTIAN COMMUNITY LEADERS. (And we are appealing to them to come forth.) We set forth this clear understanding that, for two hundred years, our Christian church failed on its stance.

Actions

What is God's people's primary source of service?

Thy word is a lamp unto my feet, and a light unto my path. I Have sworn, and I will perform it, that I will keep thy righteous judgment. (Psalm 119:105–106)

AS FOR CHRISTIAN LEADERSHIP, THERE IS A TWO-HUNDRED-YEAR FAILURE: "I have sworn, and I will perform it, that I will keep Thy righteous judgment." THEIR FAILURE DURING THOSE TWO HUNDRED YEARS WAS THAT THEY WERE HANGING BLACK PEOPLE AND BURNING THEM IN THE PRESENCE OF THEIR CHILDREN, WHICH TAUGHT HATE. AND THEY PRODUCED A GENERATION OF KILLERS THAT FORMED WHITE SUPREMACY ORGANIZATIONS BUILT ON HATE. THE CHRISTIAN LEADERSHIP HAS DONE NOTHING TO INFORM THE CHURCH

ABOUT THAT PROBLEM BECAUSE THEY ARE CHIL-
DREN OF THE CHURCH.

> Who knowing the judgment of God, that they
> which commit such things are worthy of death,
> not only do the same, but have pleasure in them
> that do them. (Romans 1:32)

GOD HAS PROMISED TO BRING GREAT TRIBU-
LATION UPON THIS LAST GENERATION. Most people
today believe that it will be a long time before the coming of Christ,
and they do not need to worry about any of that.

But we set forth clear details in *picture D*, explaining the coming of Christ, and if you study this book, you will see that this is the
last generation. This is why we are preaching out. Over time, the
devil has gained control over this generation. Church leaders work
harder with the president and lobbyists to control the country's circumstances, ignoring the will of God.

In prophecy, we are close to the time of the opening of the
six seals, which is God's anger released upon the world. THIS IS,
IN PART, THE REASON FOR WRITING THIS BOOK.
PURSUANT TO ZECHARIAH 5:1, THE FLYING ROLL
WILL BE RELEASED BY GOD ACROSS THE FACE OF
THIS EARTH.

AND AT THAT TIME, IF A MAN IS LIVING HOLY,
HE WILL CONTINUE TO LIVE HOLY. BUT IF HE IS
LIVING UNHOLY, HE WILL CONTINUE TO LIVE
UNHOLY AND BE CUT OFF FROM THE KINGDOM
OF GOD.

It's heartbreaking to reach out to this generation. Knowing that
if they will take the time to study, they will be saved BECAUSE
THE LORD HAS SAID THAT IT'S NOT HIS WILL THAT
NONE SHOULD PERISH, BUT THAT ALL SHOULD
COME UNTO THE UNITY OF THE FAITH.

God is going to bring a wreck to this world. But because most
people do not believe in the revelations, they remain unaware.

OUR BIBLICAL SCHOLARS ARE JUST AS AWARE OF THE CRITICAL PROBLEMS AS I AM, BUT I DO NOT KNOW HOW TO REACH OR ENCOURAGE THEM TO REACH OUT TO THIS LAST GENERATION.

For I have heard numerous ministers of today going forth with the word and knowing accordance with Hebrews 6:4–5.

> For it is impossible for those who were once enlightened, and have tasted of the heavenly gift, and were made partakers of the Holy Ghost.
> And have tasted the good word of God, and the power of the world to come.

WHEREAS I AM NOT GOING TO CALL ANY NAMES, IN LISTENING, I KNOW THEY ARE THE LORD'S SERVANTS. AND THAT IS THE REASON I WAS SAYING THOSE SERVANTS SHOULD BE GOING FORTH AND TEACHING THE REVELATIONS. THE TIME IS SO CLOSE, AND THE NEED IS SO GREAT.

Basically, man is only concerned about the things he can understand, and he thinks that it takes a long time for things to occur.

ALWAYS, AS I THINK MY WAY THROUGH THINGS, THE SCRIPTURES COME TO MIND.

> For my thought are not your thoughts, neither are your ways my ways, saith the Lord. For the heavens is higher that the earth, so are my ways higher that your ways, and my thoughts than your thoughts. (Isaiah 55:8, 9)

FOR EXAMPLE, THE RAPTURE COMES BEFORE THE OPENING OF THE SIX SEALS, "but the rapture occurs in the twinkle of an eye." Two things can occur at the same time. THE SIX SEALS AND THE RAPTURE CAN OCCUR AT THE SAME TIME BECAUSE A TWINKLE IS QUICKER

THAN A BLINK, SO THAT OCCURRENCE CAN HAP-
PEN QUICKLY.

The Great Tribulation: The Opening of the Six Seals

For man not to care about the revelations, he has no idea of the
wrath of God coming against the last generation. A warning from the
Lord to the church:

> Remember therefore how thou hast received and
> heard, and hold fast, and repent. If therefore thou
> shalt not watch, "I will come on thee as a thief,
> and thou shall not know what hour I will come
> upon thee." (Revelation 3:3)

LOOKING AT THE CIRCUMSTANCES, I AM
CONVINCED COVID-19 IS IN PART CONNECTED
TO PROPHECY BECAUSE IT PUTS MAN'S ATTEN-
TION TOWARD CHRIST. It is important in this last generation
because man can have a way of not wanting to be bothered, whereas
COVID-19 has man's attention.

We must realize that the wrath of God is not for the Jews only.

> And to you who are troubled rest with us, when
> the Lord Jesus shall be revealed from heaven with
> his mighty angles. In flaming fire taking ven-
> geance on them that know not God, and that
> obey not the gospel of our Lord Jesus Christ. (2
> Thessalonians 1:7–8)

WE CANNOT CLAIM TO BE IGNORANT OF THE
WILL OF GOD. HE HAS TOLD US TO STUDY. HE HAS
PROVIDED US WITH HIS WORD. HE HAS TOLD US
TO ASSEMBLE OURSELVES TO GATHER, AND WE
KNOW THAT THE WRATH OF GOD IS COMING.

For the wrath of God is revealed from heaven against all ungodliness and unrighteousness of men, who hold the truth in unrighteousness. BECAUSE THAT WHICH MAY BE KNOWN OF GOD IS MANIFEST IN THEM. FOR GOD HATH SHEWED IT UNTO THEM. FOR THE INVISIBLE THINGS OF HIM FROM THE CREATION OF THE WORLD ARE CLEARLY SEEN, BEING UNDERSTOOD BY THE THINGS THAT ARE MADE, EVEN HIS ETERNAL POWER AND GODHEAD; SO THAT THEY ARE WITHOUT EXCUSE. (Romans 1:18–20)

In my earnest deliberation to reach man, I thought it needful to set forth the above facts. "The Lord has made everything clear" and man is without excuse.

A WARNING FROM THE LORD TO THE CHURCH:

Remember therefore how thou hast received and heard, and hold fast, and repent. If therefore thou shalt not watch, I will come on thee as a thief, and thou shall not know what hour I will come upon thee. (Revelation 3:3)

If that statement has ever been important, it is important to this last generation because the wrath of God will fall upon this generation. I think about the weeping prophet.

Therefore prophesy thou against them all those words, and say unto them, The Lord shall roar from on high, and utter his voice from his holy habitation; he shall mightily roar upon his habitation; he shall give a shout, as they that tread the grapes, against all the inhabitation of the earth. A noise shall come even to the ends of the earth: for the Lord hath a controversy with the nations, he will plead with all flesh; he will give them that are wicked to the sword, saith the Lord. (Jeremiah 25:30–31)

Whereas we have no way to reach man other than this book because man doesn't seem to care about the fact that this is the last generation, and a curse is coming upon this generation.

Plus no one can honestly say what we are dealing with this virus or what end results we can expect. To clear things up, we must deal with the issue of hate.

Hate

If anyone say, "I love God," and hate his brother, he is a lie; for he who does not love his brother whom he has seen cannot love God whom he has not seen. (1 John 4:20)

Hatred stirs up strife, but love covers all offenses. (Proverbs 10:12)

Everyone who hates his brother is a murderer, and you know that no murderer has eternal life abiding in him. (1 John 3:15)

There are six things that the Lord hate, seven that are an abomination to him: haughty eyes, a lying tongue, and hands that shed innocent blood, a heart that devises wicked plans, feet that make haste to run to evil, a false witness who breathes out lies, and one who sows discord among brothers. (Proverbs 6:16–19)

Let no corrupt come out of your mouths, but only such as is good for building up, as fits the occasion, that it may give to those who hear. (Ephesians 4:29)

Whoever says he is in the light and hates his brother is still in darkness. Whoever loves his brother abides in the light, and in him there is no cause for stumbling. But whoever hates his brother is in the darkness and walk in the darkness. (1 John 2:9–19)

The Lord test the righteous, but his soul hates the wicked and the one and the one who loves violence (Psalm 11:5)

CONTINUING CONCLUSION

IN THIS BOOK, WE HAVE SET FORTH PRESIDENT TRUMP'S ACTIVITIES, AND WE BELIEVE THAT HE IS A LIAR, FRAUDULENT IN DECEIT, AND ONLY CONCERNED ABOUT HIMSELF, HIS FAMILY, AND CORRUPT FRIENDS.

And he has to be opposed, voted against, and removed because he is a sewer and the leader of hate, with 60 percent.

The wrath of God will fall upon this generation. The flying roll will be manifested during this generation, and at that time, there will be no chance of repentance.

We, as Christians, must deal with this generation. Our country is confronted with homegrown terrorism, and the commander is Norman Olson, Michigan Militia Commander.

Furthermore, President Trump is participating, as shown in the following:

@realDonaldTrump
11:22 a.m. April 17, 2020
LIBERATE MICHIGAN!

@realDonaldTrump
11:25 a.m. April 17, 2020
LIBERATE VIRGINIA and save your 2nd Amendment. It is under siege.

Words Matter

Furthermore, during the first debate, while President Trump was being questioned about homegrown terrorists, he spoke and said to them, "Step down and stay around." Once again, words matter.

IT IS EVIDENT, LOOKING AT TRUMP'S BILLS, THAT HE OWES MILLIONS OF DOLLARS COMING DUE SOON. WHEN HE LOSES THIS ELECTION, CHANCES ARE HE WILL END UP IN PRISON.

Under continuing conclusions and hate, we set forth the Lord's position.

AND IT IS FOR THIS REASON THAT ORGANIZATIONS LIKE THE WHITE NATIONALISTS SHOULD BE ADDRESSED BY THE CHURCH. CHILDREN WHO ARE NOW WHITE NATIONALISTS WERE OFFSPRING OF THE CHURCH HOUSEHOLD BECAUSE THEIR PARENTS HAVE TAKEN THEM TO HANGINGS AND BURNINGS OF BLACKS.

The conclusion as of September 9, 2020: TODAY'S MINISTRIES DO NOT ADDRESS THIS END-DAY GENERATION, AND THERE IS A NEED TO ADDRESS IT.

Chapter 1 of the book, *Battlefield of the Mind,* is titled "The Mind Is the Battlefield." It totally grasps the gravity of today's circumstances, leaving me no room to elaborate. We must confront this generation because it is the lying generation.

I KNOW THE LORD CHOSE ME TO WRITE THIS BOOK ON REVELATIONS. MY CLOSING STATEMENT IS TO THE MEN OF GOD AROUND THIS COUNTRY AND THE WORLD WHO ARE GIVING MONEY TO DONALD TRUMP. You know what kind of person Donald Trump is. He incited his people to riot on January 6 at the Capitol. Graham did everything he could to support Trump's deadly presidency, even tweeting after the election was called for Joe Biden.

Not only Graham, but there are numerous evangelists and large church heads accepting money from their members who love the Lord and pay their tithes because we are tithe payers, "giving to support the kingdom, in soul winning."

And there are many church leaders giving church money to support the devil, clinging to right-wing criminal groups. As said above, five people died in the Capitol attack, one of them a police officer. Numerous police officers were seriously injured. And the Lord is going to demand an account of you.

AFTER THE RAPTURE WHEN JESUS TAKES SAINTS AWAY

Refer to exhibits H.a and H.b.

H.a—the sun shall be darkened, and the moon shall not give her light. Neither men nor women can hear the cattle. Both the fowl of heaven and the beast have fled; they are gone.

Current Events

This book includes prophecy history and current events. Work to confirm the prophecy. Prophecy is stating what is going to happen. The current events state what has happened. One of the things that we have stated is that we are living in the last generation. The current events in 2023 are confirming that it is true.

ADDITIONAL DOCUMENTS

I.   **The Birthday of June 6, 2006**
     THY WORD IS TRUTH.
     SATAN'S BIRTHDAY: (TIMEFRAME)
     It is a fact that the devil's birthday is clearly within a timeframe, which is during the time of revelations.

THE FOLLOWING ACTIONS WERE OCCURRING AT THE TIME OF THE REVELATIONS:

THE LORD SAID THE ANTICHRIST IS GOING TO COME INTO OUR KINGDOM AND CAUSE A FALLING AWAY, AND THE MAN OF SIN SHALL BE REVEALED (2 Thessalonians 2:3). THAT WILL OCCUR DURING THE REVELATIONS. (THIS IS WHEN THE ANTICHRIST COMES ON THE SCENE.)

> He's going to come up and become strong with small people. (Daniel 11:23)

> HE SHALL COME IN PEACEABLE AND OBTAIN THE KINGDOM BY FLATTERIES. (Daniel 11:21)

The realization is that the Antichrist is on earth today. It is a revelation, according to prophecy. We set forth the actions of the Antichrist while he dwells within the beasts, which are our four nations today.

> And in latter time of their Kingdom, when the transgressors are come to full, a king of fierce countenance, and understanding dark sentences stand up. (Daniel 8:23)

THE ANTICHRIST ACTIONS WITHIN OUR FOUR-NATION KINGDOM (THE BEAST) ARE ALL OCCURRING AT THE TIME OF THE REVELATIONS.

> And though his policy also he shall cause craft to prosper in his hand; and he shall magnify himself in his heart, and by peace shall destroy many. (Daniel 8:25)

HE SHALL SCATTER AMOUNG THEM
THE PREY, AND SPOIL, AND RICHES:
YEA, AND HE SHALL FORECAST HIS
DEVICES AGAINST THE STRONG
HOLDS, EVEN FOR A TIME. (Daniel 11:24)

II. **The Leopard**

My Bible interpretation is also based on illustration. The total purpose of "the leopard" is to confirm it as the beast. God refers to the beast as listed below.

1. Colossus
2. The beast with seven heads
3. Leopard

The beasts above are set up in the order listed in my prophecy. Whereas our topic is about the leopard, we are attaching six different documents to explain the biblical interpretation of the leopard as follows:

Our God did not set forth the Bible prophecy in 1-2-3 or A-B-C order.

a. The four ruling heads of Japan (this picture sets forth the body, which is the Senate)
b. The one-world government (this picture sets forth the structure of the BODY)
c. Japan is the leopard. (Japanese ecology of the Tsushima leopard cat)
d. Japan is the leopard in Revelations 13:2
e. The history of the Soviet Union (Rise of the BEAR, the Soviet Union, Daniel 7:5)
f. The time of the kingdom of the Antichrist (the chart shows the devil ruling over the BEAST in the top left corner)
g. The time of the kingdom of Christ

1. The Colossus

    The figure that King Nebuchadnezzar saw in his dream is clearly set forth in my manuscript.
2. The Beast with Seven Heads

    PROPER ORDER OF FOLLOWING KINGDOMS:

    afterward comes the fourth kingdom, which is the feet of the Colossus.

    And I stood upon the sands of the sea, and saw a beast rise up out of the sea, having seven heads and ten horns, and upon his horns ten crowns, and upon his heads the name of blasphemy. (Revelations 13:1)

3. The Leopard

    And the beast which I saw like unto a leopard, and his feet were as the feet of a bear, and his mouth as the mouth of a lion: and the dragon gave him his power, and his seat, and great authority. (Revelations 13:2)

    This occurs in time in the kingdom of today.

    Identifies the dragon as Satan. With super authority. As "prince of this world" being casted down. (Revelations 12:9)

    How art thou fallen from heaven, O "Lucifer, son of the morning! How art thou cut down to the grown, which didst weaken the nations!" (Isaiah 14:12)

We have set forth the leopard at this point as the third leopard.

In Conclusion

I have been asked why I want to write a book. I thought about it, and as a writer, I have a long way to go. But on the other hand, in writing a book on prophecy, I would need someone who understood the prophecy.

My Sunday school book incident picture shows an angel and Jesus, and because of it, I am convinced that the Lord has a purpose for me. And writing this book explaining the prophecy is what I believe the Lord called me to do (picture #D).

AND THROUGH THE YEARS, I HAVE NOTICED THAT THERE ARE NUMEROUS SCHOLARS OUT THERE. I FOLLOWED EVERY TV PRESENTATION OUT THERE, AS THERE WERE TIMES WHEN THE SCHOLARS WOULD HAVE TV SHOWS. There is only one problem: of all the TV presentations, there was not one show or program that had taken the prophecy interpretation from 2,500 hundred years ago, with King Nebuchadnezzar of the first-world kingdom, and followed the steps, changing each world kingdom up to today, which is what our prophecy does.

If events are not followed in exact steps, things are missed.

CONCLUSION OF REVELATIONS: THE FOURTH KINGDOM

The Antichrist

Picture K. The time of the abominable ruler Satan, who is the Antichrist. He will rise and become strong with small people.

The Antichrist Will Come on the Scene before the Rapture

He will enter peacefully into the highest place in the land and rise as a vile person out of the land. He will cause man to receive the mark of the beast. There shall be a falling away as the man of sin is revealed.

And he shall confirm the covenant with many, for one week, the abomination of desolation.

He shall kill the saints, and he shall cause fire to come down from heaven; craft shall prosper in his hand.

Coming of the Lord and the 144,000

Picture L. The sealing of the 144,000—it is he that sits upon the circle of the earth, which is the coming of the Lord and the 144,000.

Resurrection of the Dry Bones in the Valley

This is the army of the Lord. At the time of the opening of the six seals, 144,000 were ordered to go to the city.

Heavenly Setting

The throne of the living God, the time of the opening of the four seals, the seven flames, and the four angles are the spirits of God.

THIS TIME IN THE PROPHECY, THERE IS AN EVENT THAT IS NOT SEEN ON EARTH. THE FOUR SEALS CAN BE RELEASED WITH NO EFFECT ON THE EARTH.

The four angles are sent to the four corners of the earth—the four horses standing before the throne.

> An end is come, the end is come: it watchets for thee; behold, it is come. (Ezekiel 7:6)

> Now I will shortly pour out my fury upon thee and accomplish my anger upon thee: and I will judge thee according to thy ways and will recompense thee for all thine abominations. (Ezekiel 7:8)

Now discussing the four horses mentioned in Ezekiel (sent to hurt the earth), the four horsemen were sent to the four corners of the earth.

The Wrath of God Released upon This Earth

> Therefore prophesy and say unto them Thus saith the Lord God, Behold O my people, I will open your graves and cause you to come up out of your graves, and bring you into the land of Israel. (Ezekiel 37:12)

Time of the Opening of the Seven Seals

Picture L shows the time of the opening of the seven seals, and the scriptures set forth events that will occur and be seen upon this earth.

Picture M sets forth the opening of the seven seals, and events occurring in that picture will be seen upon this earth as occurring at this time.

Picture N is the battle of Armageddon, the great white throne, the new heaven and a new earth, Armageddon, and the heavenly Jerusalem.

Pictures H.a and *H.b* are things that will come to pass after Jesus takes his people away from the rapture.

Jesus Takes His People in the Catching Away, "Rapture"

> Now will I shortly pour out my fury upon thee, and accomplish my anger upon thee, and I will judge thee according to thy ways, and will recompense thee for all thine abomination. (Ezekiel 7:8)

> The sun shall be darkened, and the moon shall not give her light, and the stars shall fall

from heaven, and the power of heaven shall be shaken.

Neither can men hear the voice of the cattle anymore, both the fowl of the heaven and the beast are fled, they are gone.

There shall be no grapes on the vine, nor figs on the tree, and the leaf shall fade, and all the things that I have given them shall pass away.

The field is wasted, the land mourns, for the corn is wasted, the new wine is dried up, the oil languishes, the wheat and palm tree also, and the apple tree, even all the trees of the field are withered.

And I will show wonders in the heavens, and in the earth, blood and fire and pillars of smoke.

The sun shall be turned into darkness, and the moon into blood, before the great and terrible day of the Lord comes.

The sun and the moon shall be darkened, and the stars shall withdraw their shining.

THE MEAT SHALL BE CUT OFF BEFORE YOUR EYES, yea joy and gladness from the house of our God.

THE SEEDS ARE ROTTEN UNDER THEIR CLODS, THE GARDENS ARE LAID DESOLATE, THE BARNS ARE BROKEN DOWN, FOR THE CORN IS WITHERED.

The beast groans, the herds of cattle are perplexed, yea the flocks of sheep are made desolate.

Then the Lord said, I will not feed you, that that die, let it die, and that that is cut off, let it be cut off, and let the rest, eat everyone the flesh of another.

Now to those who are not concerned about their salvation, or the will of God, know this that the wrath of God will deal with you.

TEACHING OUTLINE

Discuss each, like evaluation, through truth and fact.

A. The Flying Roll
B. Truth and Fact

The purpose of this teaching outline is to clarify and prevent confusion. Because of the two issues in studying the prophecy, one can say that it is unintelligible. Define unintelligible: impossible to understand, not intelligible.

1. *The Flying Roll* is our book, which is for the purpose of winning souls.
2. Truth and facts are the foundational basis for the book.

It is impossible to teach a class if you allow the students to lie and play lying games.

I. Teaching the prophecy (A, above, and on the glide line of B above) to today's generation is our only plan. Our book's purpose is to teach prophecy, whereas we are living in the lying generation while writing this book.

II. THE LYING GENERATION IS THE THIRD ISSUE. Why should a generation be addressed as such?

1. They make mistakes, and when they hear or look at the statement, they do not like its comparison to the truth.

2. They are in an election and have made other statements that they do not all agree with.
3. They have formed a group to support them in whatever way they become involved.
4. It could be President Trump, who believes he never makes a mistake or a lie.

III. The basis of this teaching outline is needed to avoid confusion because some issues are difficult to understand. The prophecy and lying generation are the issues.

If we are liars, we attach ourselves to the devil, because he is a liar, and the father of it. (John 8:44)

IV. Based upon the two issues and the circumstances being set forth in writing this book, the circumstances are: starting the book with the prophecy, then moving on to instructions and the teaching of current events. That scheduling process will follow, though, in the complete writing of this book.

V. FURTHERMORE, TRUTH AND FACT CANNOT BE SEPARATED.

1. It is impossible to connect "lie and fact." Therefore, we are setting forth "truth and fact."
2. We are seeking to establish "proof and truth."

It is extremely difficult when you are living in a "lying generation." Why do I say that it is a lying generation? It is because we have a president who will make a recorded TV statement and, the next day, give the opposite recorded TV statement. And he has a 35 percent following of voters, which claim that he "never lies." This forces us to confirm the proof and truth in everything.

Facts

IT WOULD BE FAR EASIER TO WRITE THIS BOOK, WITH LESS TIME SPENT DEALING WITH CONFRONTING ISSUES, IF WE WERE NOT CONFRONTING TRUMP'S YES-MEN.

1. Establish truth and proof as the basis of the study.
   a. The devil is not asleep; he is sending forth a message to control the mind of man! Man should take no part in unfruitful works of darkness. Because Joyce Meyer carefully and elaborately details the issues of the mind while reading the book, I see that people living in this generation of lies can benefit from reading and understanding the book. This is why we are recommending to those who don't have the book that they buy one, because that will make it easier to understand our revelation book.
   b. Because we are the lying generation, I need to define the term media/truth, because it is important to understand its effect on this book and on the entire world.
2. We could not complete this book while living in a lying generation without addressing those issues.
   a. This world is confronted with an extremely new and unbelievable problem. A "virus" came from Wuhan, China, and no one knows exactly how people become affected by it. We must mention our president again because he is still the president and the chief person in charge of the leadership of this country.
   b. As stated previously, it is impossible to connect "lie and fact."

IN TOUCHING ON THE ISSUES OF TODAY AND POLITICS, WE MUST OBSERVE SOME OF THE CIRCUMSTANCES UNDER WHICH THIS PRESIDENT BECAME PRESIDENT.

1. He made recorded statements about what he was going to do with an issue.
2. Then he would return and tell you that you did not understand what he said on the recorded statement (confusing).
3. His attorneys said the news did not know his state of mind.
4. Trump said on Fox Business News, "You know in April, it supposedly dies, with the hotter weather" (speaking of the coronavirus).
5. On February 24, Trump baselessly claimed that the situation was "under control" (another false statement).

In considering the truth and fact, there is no possibility that the issues set forth above, in 1 to 5, are true. We are forced by circumstances to confront numerous issues in world events because President Trump is such a ridiculous liar and will confront and fight you if you do not agree with his lies.

LET'S CONSIDER OTHER ISSUES IN PRESIDENT TRUMP'S LIFE.

I. Federal court approves $25 million Trump settlement.

During the lawsuit, Trump was badmouthing the judge because he was a Mexican. The statement was given on Tuesday by students who said they were duped by Donald Trump and his now-defunct Trump University, which promised to teach them the "secret of success" in the real estate industry.

No one gives away 25 million dollars to people if they weren't lying and cheating them in a court case. His 35 percent yes-men followers could not lie him out of that one.

II. Donald Trump performs his art of the deal business practices.

1. According to the *New York Times*, in an article titled "Decade in the Red: Trump Tax Figures Show Over 1

Billion in Business Losses" under "Time Investigation," newly obtained tax information reveals that from 1985 to 1994, Donald J. Trump's business was in far worse conditions than was previously known. By the time his master-of-the-unique memoir, *Trump: The Art of the Deal*, hit the bookstores in 1987, Donald J. Trump was already in deep financial distress, losing tens of millions of dollars on troublesome business deals, according to previous figures from his federal income tax returns.

2. The numbers showed that in 1985, Mr. Trump reported a loss of $46.1 million from his core businesses, largely casinos, hotels, retail spaces, and apartment buildings. They continued to lose money every year, totaling $1.17 billion in losses for the decade.

III. TRUMP REFUSED TO PAY HIS BILLS WHILE BUILDING HOTELS.

In the hotels that Mr. Trump built in 1985, he did not pay his bills to the contractors who did the construction.

1. *USA TODAY*

In a *USA TODAY* exclusive, hundreds allege that Donald Trump does not pay his bills. On June 9, 2016, he landed a $400,000 contract to build the bases for slots machines, registration desks, bars, and other cabinets at the Harrah's hotel.

Trump still owes money to contractors who built Taj Mahal casino on January 24, 2020, and what he did not tell the sources to contractors who worked on the overly large casino was that he could not pay their bill.

2. *Wall Street Journal*

Donald Trump's business plan left a trail of unpaid bills. On June 9, 2016, the best-known payment dispute was in Atlantic City in the early 1990s, when Trump's executives told contractors working on his hotels that Trump did not pay his bills (USATODAY.COM).

From I to III, Donald Trump paid a $25 million lawsuit and continued with lies, cheating, and fraud, refusing to pay contractors who worked on his hotels.

Furthermore, through his actions, lies, cheating, and fraud, he lost more than $1 billion in nine years. And with such repercussions, as president of this country, we are protecting our true prophecy, against President Trump's lies, false statements, and misrepresentations, because this book also includes COVID-19 issues occurring. (And the fact is that President Trump tells many lies about COVID-19.)

THE REASON FOR THIS "TEACHING OUT-LINE" IS THAT PRESIDENT TRUMP WAS TAKING PICTURES NEAR THE CHURCH HOLDING A BIBLE. Similarly, Adolf Hitler took a picture holding a Bible. Because, for sure, if we are not following righteousness, then we are following the path of the devil. Trump's functions are identical to Satan's.

There are things set forth on the first page of this book.

1. The Flying Roll
2. Truth and Fact
3. The Lying Generation

In part, the purpose of this teaching outline is **clarification**. There is no reason today's Bible scholars are not doing revelation interpretations. It is extremely difficult to avoid confusion in the explanation.

Foundation and Basic Two Steps for Book Study

The foundation and efforts upon which the book is based are as follows:

1. Truth
2. Fact

The reason we examine President Trump's history, in I to III, in this teacher's outline is to determine the type of person we are dealing with in relation to "truth and fact." It is impossible to ignore him because he is talking on TV daily, wanting to be in control of everything.

The fact is that, for sure, if we are not following righteousness, then we are following the path of the devil. Trump's functions are identical to Satan's.

Get an Understanding

1. Understanding is defined as a psychological process related to an abstract or physical object, such as a person, situation, or message, whereby one can think about it and use concepts to deal adequately with that object. Understanding is a relationship between the knower and the object of understanding.

2. The Bible

    And I have filled him with the spirit of God, in wisdom, and in understanding, and in knowledge, and in all manner of workmanship. (Exodus 31:3)

    And God gave Solomon wisdom and exceedingly great understanding, and largeness of heart like the sand of the seashore. Thus, Solomon's wisdom excelled the wisdom of all men. (1 Kings 4:29)

Now we know from the above observation of the word *understanding* that God gave Solomon understanding, and in our study, "we must pray God for understanding" while studying the prophecy. FURTHERMORE, TRUTH AND FACT CANNOT BE SEPARATED. It is impossible to connect "lie and fact." Therefore, we are setting forth truth and fact.

Jesus says, "If you abide in my word, you are truly my disciples. And you will know the truth, and the truth will set you free." (John 8:31–32)

The Three Comings of Christ

(At this point, we are only dealing with coming number one.)

1. The "Marriage Supper of the Lamb," Jesus on this coming, is the bridegroom.
2. THE STONE THAT WAS CUT OUT WITHOUT HANDS IS THE KINGDOM OF GOD STRIKING THE BEAST (THE NATIONS OF TODAY). The beast is also the feet. The bottom of picture A shows the kingdom of God striking the ONE-WORLD GOVERNMENT—THE BEAST. GOD FORETOLD 2,500 YEARS AGO THAT JESUS'S COMING KINGDOM WOULD DESTROY THE BEAST.
3. The one-world kingdom of today means the kingdom of God will be striking the four-world nations of today. It's hard for us to imagine that, but that is what God has said, and it's going to happen in today's generation. One of the world's organizations will have a part in that.

CONTENTS AT A GLANCE

We are examining the stone.

Part I: Three Divisions of the Book

1. Teaching Outline
2. Contents Briefly
3. Prophecy—Different Times in the Prophecy

Part II. Details of the Three Divisions of the Book

Prophecy (number 3)

We're attempting to establish where we are now in time "in relation to the stone." Through the prophecy and the word of God, we have proven that we are down to the last four kingdoms of man.

FURTHERMORE, THE LORD SET FORTH IN THE REVELATIONS WHAT THE END EVENTS WOULD BE. It is necessary to introduce some facts involving the end-time prophecy (this will establish a point in time for the prophecy). To establish proof, the last four nations now exist—England, the USA, the USSR, and Japan/China.

a. THE STONE WAS CUT OUT WITHOUT HANDS

(*picture E*, showing the picture where the kingdom of God struck the feet of the Colossus).

b. Furthermore, the coming of the kingdom of Christ
    strikes the beast, which is the feet. WE HAVE NOT
    CONFIRMED IN SCRIPTURE, AT THIS
    POINT, WHEN THE FOUR NATIONS OF
    TODAY ESTABLISHED THEMSELVES AS
    THE ONE-WORLD GOVERNMENT.
c. The bottom of the *picture E* shows the kingdom of
    God striking the one-world government, which is also
    called the beast (the kingdom of God striking the four
    nations of today).

Part III. Further Details of the Third Portion of the Book

1. In discussing the one-world government, there are
    issues that are incomplete. For example, Russia has
    been removed from the G7 World Association.
2. This means they could not vote to form the world's
    nations into a one-world government, but President
    Trump has recommended that Russia be reinstated.
3. And it is our question: Where are we in prophecy?
    Will Russia be reinstated?

DIFFERENT WORDS HAVE THE SAME MEANING.

1. Feet
2. Government
3. Beast

Because of this prophecy!

They shall mingle themselves with the seeds of
men: but they shall not cleave one to another.
(Daniel 2:43)

THE SCRIPTURES ABOVE MENTION DEMONIC BEINGS MINGLING THEMSELVES WITH THE SEED OF MEN. NOW THAT IS A SITUATION THAT WILL OCCUR IN THE ONE-WORLD GOVERNMENT. The one-world government is also displayed as "the beast with seven heads."

Refer to *picture B* of this book displaying the beast with seven heads (that picture is based upon "biblical interpretations").

Doing the interpretations: Beast = kingdom, government, and political power.

The beast is defined on the content sheet of this book.

SO NOW WE KNOW THAT THE KINGDOM OF GOD IS HITTING AND DESTROYING A "GOVERNMENT." AND THESE ARE THE FOLLOWING:

1. England
2. USA
3. USSR
4. a. Japan
   b. China

These four nations are a **government**—one-world government.

We are seeking to establish at what point in time in this generation some of those events will happen.

We placed additional exhibits in this book because it is a book of prophecy, which requires a considerable explanation.

Appendix A

My Chapter Checklist

Issues Involved around COVID-19

I.   Because this book is a prophecy, highlighting the details of the issues is important. In the first paragraph of this book, we set forth an issue—COVID-19. Why is it important to mention the virus in this book?

  Because our goal is to win souls, and we need an honest opportunity among the population because, in this country, we have a president. He is on TV, talking daily. He wants to be in control of everything and believes that he never makes a mistake and that he never lies.

  Therefore, in order to proceed with our book, we must confront the president, whose issues are lying, cheating, abusing, misleading, and confusing people.

  All over the world, people are giving their lives to Christ, and we do not know how close we are to the end times. But we want every honest effort possible to win everyone.

II. At this point in time, we must include politics because of the reasons we set forth above about the president.

  BECAUSE POLITICS PLAY AN IMPORTANT ROLE IN OUR LIVES, ALL ASPECTS OF OUR LIVES CONCERNING THE VIRUS ARE INVOLVED IN POLITICS, AND BECAUSE OF

COVID-19, WE ARE IN A FIGHT THAT IS A WORLDWIDE PROBLEM. Furthermore, because we are in the 2020 election and doing an election, politics and lies are commonplace.

III. These are today's circumstances.

These days, it is impossible not to include politics, which involves trust and proof. The fact is that the president knew about the virus in January first, or no later than January 10, yet he made no effort to go forth as our president in providing for us. What he was doing was constantly saying things about the virus. It was being done by the Democrats to give him a black eye (playing down the virus). For approximately two months, the president did nothing to protect us, not even "social distancing or any such efforts."

IV. I am disturbed when I hear on the news that, when it comes to Christian organizations, you know how they are going to vote.

The church has refused to stand for the *value of truth*, in the past and today, whereas the church is supposed to be the *pillar of truth*. (Keeping in mind that God destroyed the first world because of sin.)

Yet they refuse to speak of righteousness to the organizations upholding and supporting killing around the country. They operate according to the mind of the flesh (of which the devil is in control).

Because Joyce Meyer carefully elaborated on the details of the issues of the mind while reading the book, I could see that people living in this generation of lies could benefit from reading and understanding this book.

Which is why we are recommending to those who don't have the book yet to buy one. It would make it much easier to understand our book of prophecy.

Why are they listening to the leaders of Christian organizations? In dealing with political parties, they are often supported by and involved with organizations.

In setting forth that point, it is not just man's political decisions about politics and the different groups on radio, which include mobile radio and television, and other news agencies' *manipulation* to control the country and world issues.

I HAVE STUDIED REVELATIONS FOR FIFTY YEARS, AND I AM SEVENTY-NINE YEARS OLD, AND I AM PUSHED TO PUBLISH THIS BOOK.

WE HAVE SET FORTH SCRIPTURAL PROOF, THE END IS NEAR, AND WE ARE UNDER THE SIEGE OF COVID-19.

V.   That is why God destroyed the first world.

AND TODAY'S ORGANIZATIONS ARE BUILT UPON HATE, WANT TO KILL AND GENERATE FEAR, AND HAVE GIVEN NO THOUGHT TO FACTS AS TO WHERE THEY ARE GOING TO SPEND ETERNITY. And the people we are talking about are supposed to be Christian people's children.

VI. We have taken a hard stand on the truth.

"Because the weapons of our warfare are not carnal, but mighty though God to the pulling down of strong holds."

But if I tarry long, that thou mayest know how thou ought to believe thyself in the house of God, which is the church of the living God, PILLAR and GROUND of the TRUTH. (1 Timothy 3:15)

The devil is betting Christians to death, and for the past two hundred years, Christians have produced a prejudice-killing generation of Christians with no thoughts about where they are going to spend eternity.

VII. The flying roll is when God sends forth a curse across the face of the earth.

1. The beginning's teaching is prophecy, whereas we are living in a lying generation while writing this book.
2. The lying generation is a third issue.
    Why should a generation be addressed as such?

    a. They make statements, and when they hear or look at the statement, they do not like the way it is compared to the truth.
    b. They are in an election and have made other statements, which do not all agree.

Current Events

During the spread of the virus, the church was closed. I was traveling through my neighborhood and noticed a church near my home. I thought that was a good thing. And when we were allowed again to tend the church, we attended that new church, Love Land Church, with Pastor Chuck Singleton. Pastor Singleton's message is, "Love wins a place" (Matthew 25:36–40).

James Reston of the *New York Times* captured Lyndon Baines Johnson on the day of his inauguration in 1965. Here was a man speaking of both the faith of the old frontier and the new frontier of science.

There is a gift—in fact, a giftedness—rarely seen in a church in America: the ability to have a solid foundation and soaring vision at the same time. Many believers are too afraid, while others may be too daring. Some won't try anything, while others will try everything. The connection between the maturity of our past doubts and the majesty of a glorious future has one thing between the two, which may get in the way. Suit yourself. What Mr. Reston saw in President

Johnson was a man who had not forgotten where he had come from and yet had an urge to go where he had never been.

What I am making a point about is that we live in a generation of **lies** and **killings**, totally rejecting love.

We earlier explained that Trump is the person causing the great falling away in the revelation spoken of by the Bible: "Six hundred thousand people turn from following Christ to following Trump."

"Further, the fear leaves us when we understand that we are not alone. When we can see the hand of God guiding, protecting, and equipping us, we are emboldened to go forward!"

WHAT IS THE RECENT DAMAGE TO THIS WORLD FROM CLIMATE CHANGE?

Droughts, floods, and record-low ice levels—from the top of the world's mountains to the depths of the ocean—the climate crisis took a heavy toll as it continued to intensify in 2022, a new analysis from the World Meteorological Organization shows.

CNN states that the world failed its health checkup.

1. Ocean heat hits another record high in 2022, fueling extreme weather.
2. The world's oceans were the warmest on record for the fourth year in a row in 2022, a troubling sign of the climate crisis caused by humans pumping heat-trapping gases into the atmosphere.
3. The world isn't moving fast enough to cut pollution and keep warming below 2 degrees Celsius, the UN scorecard says.
4. Global CO_2 emissions from fossil fuels will rise by less than 1 percent this year as renewables and EVs take off (related article).

Exhibits

Because this book is about prophecy, these exhibits are included to provide information for any and all documents in support of proof for the document.

1. Colossus (*picture A*): Picture showing the image King Nebuchadnezzar saw in his dream
2. Four beasts
3. Picture listing all world governments
4. One-page map (*picture C*)
5. Antichrist came out of one of the five divisions of Alexander's kingdom

In Conclusion

In 2023, there are numerous serious issues confronting us and a problem controlling the issues.

DEMOCRATIC-HYPOCRISY

The said terms are indicative of the majority of the problems. For example,

- Democratic—the main enforcers are the USA, England, France, Scotland, and so forth.
- Hypocrisy—the main enforcers are Russia, China, Iran, and the United Arab Emirates.

Because of the warring factions between those two, there is no hope for the world to gather and be on one accord to resolve our major world issues.

World Financial Problems

Numerous countries are involved in finding the best method to use cryptocurrency. They are looking for the best method to involve themselves.

1. **Cryptocurrency is a big issue in finance.**
   Most nations around the world are involved in finding the best method to put themselves in to deal with cryptocurrency. Britain sets out plans to regulate cryptocurrencies. The proposal includes strengthening the rules for the cryptocurrency industry.

2. **EU is close to introducing groundbreaking laws to regulate cryptocurrency on October 27, 2020.**
   In October 2022, the European Council approved the markets in crypto (MICA) regulations, one of the first attempts globally at comprehensive regulations of the cryptocurrency market. The regulations extend to money laundering. The European Union (9EU) is a pioneer in digital regulations, and the breadth of MICA means that it will have a significant global impact.

3. **UK Parliament tries cryptocurrency.**
   The government announced its plan for the UK to become a global hub for the crypto and digital asset industries. Since then, it has introduced legislation that will support the use of one type of cryptocurrency—backed stablecoin—as a form of payment. In February 2023, it launched a consultation to develop a new regulatory regime for the crypto sector.

4. **IS THE US DOLLAR GOING TO GO DIGITAL?**
   The Feds are still evaluating the potential impact of a digital dollar. It currently has several studies, pilot tests, and experiments underway to determine the technology's opportunities and limitations.

Farella says the Feds may opt to create a digital dollar that is not a pure CBDC but rather a public-private hybrid currency. Whitehouse considers creating a digital dollar. The Biden administration is exploring the idea of creating a digital currency for the US, saying it could help strengthen the nation's role as a global financial leader. Today, it released a framework outlining the regulation of digital assets, including cryptocurrency and other items of value that exist only in digital form. The framework includes ways to make the handling of these assets easier and ensure that the digital asset space is resistant to fraud.

President Biden is currently working to create development assets through his Executive Order 14067.

5. **GREAT BRITAIN'S INVOLVEMENT IN CRYPTOCURRENCY—Is the UK a global hub?**

The UK is the heart of the world's financial market. With unrivaled access to global markets, the UK is the world's most open and connected financial center. We have an inspiring ecosystem where your business can then thrive. We're here, and we're ready to do business with you.

The capital of the United Kingdom is home to 8.9 million residents, 50 bitcoin ATMs, and about the same number of merchants who will accept bitcoin for payment. Startups based in the city include Coinfloor, which claims to be the oldest bitcoin exchange in the UK. There are also dozens of bitcoins and cryptocurrency meetup groups in London.

How to Measure Bitcoin Adoption

1. San Francisco
2. Vancouver
3. Amsterdam
4. Ljubljana
5. Tel Aviv

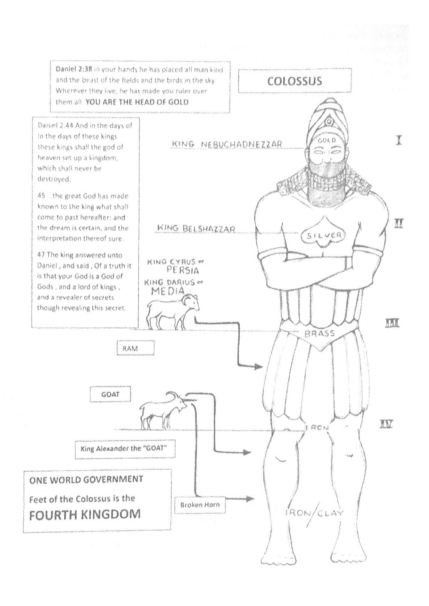

Daniel 2:38 in your hands he has placed all man kind and the beast of the fields and the birds in the sky Wherever they live, he has made you ruler over them all. **YOU ARE THE HEAD OF GOLD**

Daniel 2.44 And in the days of In the days of these kings these kings shall the god of heaven set up a kingdom, which shall never be destroyed:

45 ...the great God has made known to the king what shall come to past hereafter: and the dream is certain, and the interpretation thereof sure.

47 The king answered unto Daniel , and said , Of a truth it is that your God is a God of Gods , and a lord of kings , and a revealer of secrets though revealing this secret.

COLOSSUS

KING NEBUCHADNEZZAR

GOLD   I

KING BELSHAZZAR

SILVER   II

KING CYRUS of PERSIA
KING DARIUS of MEDIA

RAM

BRASS   III

GOAT

King Alexander the "GOAT"

IRON   IV

ONE WORLD GOVERNMENT

Feet of the Colossus is the

FOURTH KINGDOM

Broken Horn

IRON/CLAY

116

THIS DOCUMENT ILLUSTRATE INFORMATION WHICH SET FORTH THE RISE OF ENGLAND TO WORLD POWER

KING THEODOSIUS GRANTED THE VISIGOTH KINGSHIP THAT AUTHORITY. IN 382 B.C.

Theodosius I
379–395

East

Arcadius
395–408

Theodosius II
408–450

West

Honorius
395–423

Johannes (usurper)
423–425

Valentinian III
425–455

Ivory plaque showing the emperor Honorius. The nimbus around his head carries the dedication 'To our Lord Honorius the Eternal Emperor'

378. Valens himself was killed along with most of his high command and enormous numbers of troops.

The Theodosian Dynasty

When Valens was killed at Hadrianopolis it fell to the then western emperor Gratian to take measures for the defence of the east. This he did by appointing Flavius Theodosius, a Spanish officer, as emperor for the eastern provinces on 19 January 379. Theodosius proved a redoubtable figure in both civil and military affairs, and came to be called 'the Great'. He was particularly noted as a law-giver and an ardent defender of Christianity. In 391 he at long last brought to completion the official espousal of Christianity by forbidding pagan worship, whether public or private, and closing all pagan temples. Yet he himself ran foul of the religion in 390 when he was excommunicated by Ambrose bishop of Milan for ordering the massacre of the citizens of Thessalonica who had murdered his army commander. Only when he had done penance was he allowed back into the fold.

Theodosius settled the military situation in the east by a four-year war against the Goths, ending in a peace treaty in 382. This set a disturbing precedent by allowing the Visigoths to settle on lands within the empire under the authority of their own kings rather than any imperial official, and the right to fight in the Roman army as allies rather than regular units. Theodosius may have hoped to establish firmer control once the immediate crisis had passed, but the opportunity never came. Indeed the most conspicuous military operations of Theodosius's reign were in the west. It was he who led the army to Italy which defeated Magnus Maximus in 388, and in a second campaign in 394 overthrew Eugenius and Arbogast, murderer of Valentinian II.

Honorius's reign was dominated by Germanic incursions. In 401 the Visigoths whom Theodosius had settled in Thrace moved westward under Alaric their king and raided northern Italy. They were driven back by Stilicho, Honorius's army commander, but other Germanic peoples entered Italy in 405, and in December 406 Vandals, Sueves and Alans crossed the frozen Rhine to ravage Gaul. Four years later, in 410, the unthinkable happened, when Alaric entered Italy once again and sacked Rome. The imperial court had by now established itself at Ravenna, a near impregnable city on the Adriatic, but the fall of Rome was nonetheless a milestone in the dissolution of the western empire.

KING ALEXANDER AS THE GREAT HORN THAT WAS BROCKEN

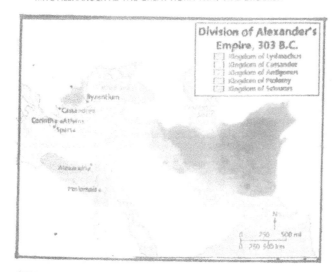

Division of Alexander's Empire. 303 B.C.

Following the death of Alexander the Great in 323 B.C., his successors
competed for his throne. After numerous battles and shifts of
allegiance, the empire was divided up among five of Alexander's generals

King Alexander's Death at 323 B.C., is clear indication that is before the coming of Christ, and
no nation did rise at that time, and continued in world power until today, to comply with the
following scriptures.

Daniel 8:8,23

8 Therefore the he goat waxed very great: and when he was strong, the great horn was broken;
and for it came up four notable ones toward the four winds of the heaven.

23 And in the latter time of their kingdom, when the transgressors are come to the full, a king
of fierce countenance, and understanding dark sentence, shall stand up.

THAT REFERENCE IS MADE OF THE ANTICHRIST, WILL COME OUT OF
ONE OF THE FOUR RISEN KINGDOMS.

http://go.hrw.com/hrw.nd/gohrw_rls1/pKeywordResults?keyword=st9%20alexander

Dan. 8:21 JULIUS CAESAR the FIRST KING of ROME

The Triumvirate and Julius Caesar

The End of Repubic-Caesar Political life

Rome Chushed Greece in 145 BC

The Rise of Rome to WORLD
POWER in Julius Caesar

"Symbolic BEAST"

Dan. 5:25 God saw Media and Persia
as ONE KINGDOM, the ram with two Kings,
and God saw Greece and Rome as one
Kingdom, The GOAT, Greece as the Great
 Horn being Rome, God
referred to ROME as the first king, which
history proved to be Julius Caesar.

And Rome rose to world power under Julius CAESAR
and in the passing of time Rome World Power ended
under Theodosius II 382.

The Kingship of ROME started with Julius Caesar and ended with King Theodosius 382 B.C.
when the GREAT HORN was broken.

D

History of Anglo-Saxon England

From Wikipedia, the free encyclopedia

The **history of Anglo-Saxon England** covers the history of England from the end of Roman Britain and the establishment of Anglo-Saxon kingdoms in the fifth century until the Norman conquest of England in 1066. Anglo-Saxon is a general term that refers to tribes of *German* origin who came to Britain, including Angles, Saxons, Frisians and Jutes.

Contents

- 1 Historical context
- 2 Sources
- 3 Migration and the formation of kingdoms (400–600)
- 4 Heptarchy and Christianisation (7th and 8th centuries)
    - 4.1 Anglo-Saxon England heptarchy
    - 4.2 Other minor kingdoms and territories
- 5 Viking challenge and the rise of Wessex (9th century)
- 6 English unification (10th century)
- 7 England under the Danes and the Norman conquest (978–1066)
    - See also
    - Notes
- 10 References
- 11 External links

Historical context

Main articles: Sub-Roman Britain and Roman departure from Britain

As the Roman occupation of Britain was coming to an end, Constantine III withdrew the remains of the army, in reaction to the barbarian invasion of Europe.[1][2] The Romano-British leaders were faced with an increasing security problem from sea borne raids, particularly by Picts on the East coast of England.[3] The expedient adopted by the Romano-British leaders was to enlist the help of Anglo-Saxon mercenaries (known as foederati), to whom they ceded territory.[3][4] In about AD 442 the Anglo-Saxons mutinied, apparently because they had not been paid.[5] The British responded by appealing to the Roman commander of the Western empire Aetius for help (a document known as the *Groans of the Britons*), even though Honorius, the Western Roman Emperor, had written to the British *civitas* in or about AD 410 telling them to look to their own defence.[6][7][8][9] There then followed several years of fighting between the British and the Anglo-Saxons.[9] The fighting continued until around AD 500.

ALFRED the GREAT
ENGLAND FIRST NATION TO RISE TO WORLD POWER AT
ALEXANDLER'S DEATH

King Alexander Died 303 B.C. and it is evident evens mentioned above could not have occurred in that time frame. NOT POSSIBLE FOR KING ALEXANDER TO BE THE GREAT HORN.

ENGLAND FIRST NATION TO RISE TO WORLD POWER AT ALEXANDER'S DEAFTH

Daniel 8:8,22 **WHEN THE GREAT HORN WAS BROKEN**

8 Therefore the he goat waxed very great: and when he was strong the great horn was broken, and for it came up four notable ones toward the four winds of the heavens 22 Now that was broken, whereas four stood up for it, four kingdoms shall stand up out of the nations .....23 And in the later times of their kingdom, when the transgressor are come to full, a king of fierce countenance, and understanding dark sentences, shall stand up.   24 And his power shall be mighty, but not by his own power: and he shall destroy wonderfully, and shall prosper, and practices, and shall destroy the mighty and the holy people.

The Kingdom of the ancestral English, Anglo-Saxon which was carved out of the former Roman province of Britannia.

United States of America U.S.A.

BELOW IS THE EMBLEM

The U.S.A is one of the last four
world powr nations at the fall of Rome

The U.S.A. is one of the nations struck by
the stone that was cut out withouy hands

It will also be one of the nations that will help
form the ONE WORLD GOVERNMENT.

THE U.S.A. will stand as a world power until the take over of tthe
ANT-CHRIST

History of the Soviet Union

History of the Soviet Union, (1917)-1927
from the October Revolution to Stalin's
consolidation of power.

Soviet Union

History of the Soviet Union(1927-1953,
the Stalin era.
History of the Soviet Union(1953-1985),
from destalinization to perestroika.
Hiatory of the Soviet Union, ended-by
dissolution.

It is one of the nations that was srtuck
by the stone cut out without hands.

THE SOVIET UNION IS LISTED IN PROPHECY AS ONE OF THE LAST FOUR
RULING WORLD GOVERNMENTS

It is considered as (U.S.S.R. Feet of the bear)

Ħ

Japan is the leopard in revelations 13:2

Daniel 7:3 Which states, FOUR BEAST shall come forth "diverse", which is
defined to mean (in this order), one after the other.

LOOK AT THE LEOPARD

National Endangered Species Tsushima Leopard Cat

Japanese Leopard

The Leopard is the symbolic Animal of Japan, it is
considered to be Lucky.

What is the Tsushima leopard cat?

The Tsushima cat is an endangered wildcat inhabiting Tsushima Islands, Nagasaki prefecture. It is
regarded as a subspecies of the leopard and is thought to have arrived in Tsushima from the Asian
continent about 100,00 years ago. The population of the Tsushima leopard cat has been declining mainly
due to habitat degradation by the Japanese goverment as a National Nature Monument in 1971 and as a
National Endangered Species in 1994. A conservation project plan was established in 1995 to protect the
species, under the direction of the ministry of the environment in conjunction with other governments
agencies.

USA
Leader of JAPAN
Leader of CHINA
British
COMMONWEALTH

THE FOUR RULING HEADS OF JAPAN

Japan is the Senate in the one-world government. (Daniel 7:6)

Four Wings
Senate
The Body

British Commonwealth Occupation Force

British Commonwealth Occupation Force (BCOF) was the name of the joint Australian, British indian Army and New Zealand military forces in occupied Japan, from 21 February 1946 until the end of occupation in 1952. At its peak bcof comprised about 40,000 personnel equal to 25% of the number of US military personnel in japan.

For most of the occsupation period

Australia contributed the majority of the BCOF's personnel. The Initial BCOF presence included the Australian 34th Infantry Brigade, Indian 268th Brigade,and the 2nd New Zealand Expeditionary Force (in J-Force). The position of commanding officer was always filled by Australians: Lt Gen. John Northcott, February to June 1946; Lt Gen Horace Robertson, June 1946 to Novemeber 1951, and; Lt Gen. William Bridgeford from November 1951 until the end of the occupation.

THe Keys Being turned over to (BCOF)

The British Pacific Fleet initially provided most of the naval forces. The air contingent, known as BCAIR initially comprised the Royal Australian Air Force No. 81 Fighter Wing, flying P-51 Mustangs, four Spitfiresquadrons (including No. 11 and No. 17 of the Royal Air Force and No. 4 of the Indian Air Force flying F4U Corsair.

THE TIME OF THE ONE WORLD GOVERNMENT

TIME OF THE BEAST

The Rise of the ANTI-CHRIST Dan7 24-Dan 8 8

Define the BEAST

THE WOUNDED HEAD OF THE BEAST IS HEALED

When the World Governments of Today are formed into a single World Government ruling the Entire WORLD.

The FORTH KINGDOM

EMPEROR-the HEAD ENGLAND and U S A

the ONE WORLD GOVERNMENT is the BEAST

JAPAN

RUSSIA

DEFINE the MARK of the Beast

TEN GOVERNORS

This point in time our plastic cards . ATM and ECT. are replacing CASH.

1 2 3 4 5 6 7 8 9 10

Dan 2:44 in the days of those kings shall

Daniel 7 24 And the 10 horns out of the kingdom are 10 kings that shall rise and

the God of heaven set up a kingdom

another shall rise after them, and he shall be diverse from the first

which shall never be destroyed

ANTI-CHRIST

THE FEET of the COLOSSUS

The forth kingdom

The FEET of the COLOSSUS -REBORN ROMAN EMPIRE

Dan 7:24 . and 10 horns are 10 kings that shall rise, after them shall rise another, and shall subdue 3 kings and shall wear out the saints

OVER 2500 YEARS AGO GOD NAMED EVERY WORLD GOVERNMENT FROM THE FIRST WORLD KINGDOM OF KING NEBUCHEDNEZZAR UNTIL THE COMING KINGDOM OF CHRIST.

Dan 1.5   Dan 2.37

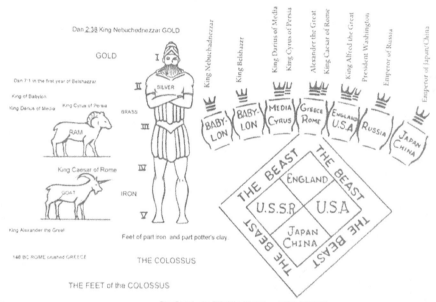

The Beast with SEVEN HEADS and TEN HORNS

THE ONE WORLD GOVERMENT

Rev. 13:2 And the BEAST which I saw was like
a LEOPARD and his FEET were as the FEET of
a BEAR, and his MOUTH as the MOUTH of a LION,
and the DRAGON gave him his POWER and SEAT, and
GREAT AUTHORITY.

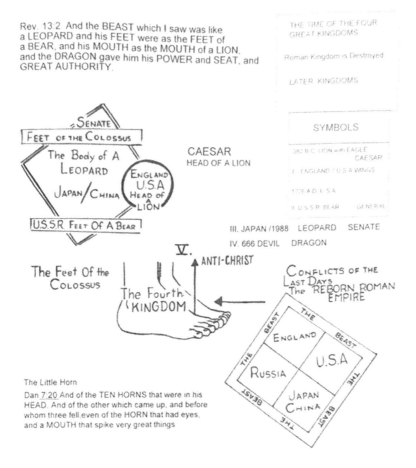

THE TIME OF THE FOUR
GREAT KINGDOMS

Roman Kingdom is Destroyed

LATER KINGDOMS

SYMBOLS

382 B.C. LION with EAGLE
                         CAESAR

I. ENGLAND / U.S.A WINGS

1776 A.D. U.S.A

II. U.S.S.R. BEAR   GENERAL

SENATE

FEET OF THE COLOSSUS

The Body of A
LEOPARD

JAPAN / CHINA

ENGLAND
U.S.A
HEAD of
A
LION

U.S.S.R. FEET OF A BEAR

CAESAR
HEAD OF A LION

III. JAPAN /1988   LEOPARD   SENATE

IV. 666 DEVIL   DRAGON

V.

ANTI-CHRIST

The Feet Of the
COLOSSUS

The Fourth
KINGDOM

CONFLICTS OF THE
LAST DAYS
The REBORN ROMAN
EMPIRE

THE BEAST

ENGLAND

THE BEAST

RUSSIA

U.S.A

THE

JAPAN
CHINA

THE BEAST

The Little Horn

Dan 7:20 And of the TEN HORNS that were in his
HEAD. And of the other which came up, and before
whom three fell, even of the HORN that had eyes,
and a MOUTH that spike very great things

131

The One World Government

The TIME of the FOUR GREAT

KINGDOMS

Rev. 13:2 And the BEAST which I saw was like

A LEOPARD and his FEET were as the FEET of   Roman Kingdom is Destroyed

a BEAR, and his MOUTH as the MOUTH of a   LATER KINGDOMS--------

:

LION: and the DRAGON gave him his POWER   SYMBOLS

And SEAT, and GREAT AUTHORITY.   382 B.C. LION with EAGEL   CAESAR

The FEET of the COLOSSUS SENATE   CAESAR   I ENGLAND & U.S.A. WINGS

       The Body of a   ENGLAND/   HEAD of a LION   1776 A.D. U.S.A.

    LEOPARD   U.S.A.   II. U.S.S.R. BEAR   GENERALAL

     JAPAN/CHINA   III. JAPAN/1988 LEOPARD SENBATE

   U.S.S.R. -RUSSIA feet of a BEAR   IV. 666 DEVIL   DRAGON

The FEET of the COLOSSUS   CONFLICKS of the LAST DAYS

The FORTH KINGDOM   The REBORN ROMAN EMPIRE

                           THE FORTH KINGDOM

The Little Horn

"Dan. 7:20 And of the TEN HORNS that were in his HEAD,

And of the other which came up, and before whom three

Fell; even of that HORN that had eyes, and a MOUTH THAT

Spike very great things, whose look was more stout than His follows."

Daniel 7:3 And the FOUR GREAT BEAST came up from the sea, diverse one from another.

Diverse one from another", "Daniel 7:4 The First was like a LOIN and had EAGEL'S WINGS.".

Daniel 7:5 And behold another BEAST a second, like to a BEAR".

Daniel 7:6 ....and lo another , like a LEOPARD, which had upon the back of it FOUR WINGS as a FOWL: the BEAST
had also FOUR HEADS and dominion was given to it.

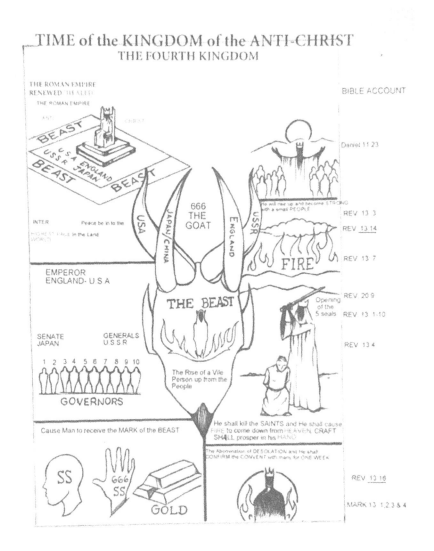

STONE CUT OUT WITHOUT HANDS

2500 YEARS AGO GOD FORETOLD THAT HIS COMING KINGDOM WORLD THE WORLD KINGDOMS OF TODAY

"Daniel 2:34 THou sawest till a STONE was cut out without hands which smote the IMAGE upon his FEET that were of

IRON and CLAY, and BRAKE them to PIECES"

"2:35   and the WIND CARRIED them AWAY. But no PLACE was found for them

and the STONE that SMOTE the IMAGE became a GREAT

MOUNTAIN and FILLED the WHOLE EARTH.

GOLD

SILVER

BRASS

IRON

STONE CUT OUT WITHOUT HANDS

IRON / CLAY

I

II

III

IV

V

Feet of part iron and part potter's clay The second image, the four nations of today, later formed into a one world government.

Chart from the fall of the ROMAN Kingdom to the establishing of CHRIST Kingdom

THE TIME OF THE COMING OF CHRIST
THE THREE COMING OF CHRIST

The RAPTURE of the CHURCH

TO THE CHURCH

Bible Access
Souls

1 Thess 4.16,17 For the Lord himself will descend from Heaven with a cry of command, with the voice of an archangel, and with the sound of the trumpet of God, and the dead in Christ will rise first.

JESUS

CHURCH

SOULS

MARRIAGE SUPPER of the LAMB

THE COMING OF CHRIST AND THE 144,000 OF THE BRIDGEROOM

LION

Zech. 14.3 Then shall the Lord go out and fight against those nations as when he fought in the days of battle
Isaiah 11.4 He shall smite the earth with the rod of his MOUTH
Joel 3.9 ... let all the men of war draw near, let them come up
3.10 Beat your plowshares into swords and your pruning hooks into spears, let the weak say I am strong

OF THE LIONS TO THE SINNERS Sound of Battle

THE EARTH

Rev 6.6, Rev 9.1

Rev 11.3,4,5

Onited Ones   Onited Ones
RIGHTOUS JUDGE

GOD OF THE EARTH

TIME of the OPENING of the FOUR SEALS

The SEVEN FLAMES and FOUR ANGELS are the SPIRITS of GOD

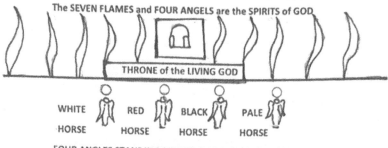

THRONE of the LIVING GOD

WHITE HORSE   RED HORSE   BLACK HORSE   PALE HORSE

FOUR ANGLES STANDING BEFORE the THRONE of GOD

WHITE SEAL	RED SEAL	BLACK SEAL	PALE SEAL
OPENED	OPENED	OPENED	OPENED

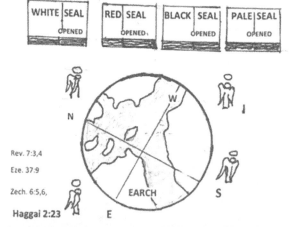

Rev. 7:3,4

Eze. 37:9

Zech. 6:5,6,

Haggai 2:23

The FOUR ANGLES SENT to the FOUR CONNERS of the EARTH and ORDERED NOT to EARTH until GOD has SEALED the 144,000 in Their FOREHEADS.

The Opening of the SEALS is the OPENING of MAN'S UNDERSTANDING to REVELATIONS

FIVE SEALS ARE NOW OPENED

MAN is without EXCUSE

The Time of the OPENING of the SEVEN SEALS

Rev. 5:1-14 Time of the   Matthew 27:52,53   FOUR SEALS are NOW

Time of the FIRST   OPENED

RESURRECTION   THE FIFTH SEAL IS ALSO

OPENING OF   is also OPENED

The FIFTH

SEAL.

Roman 1:16 For I am not ashamed

of the GOSPEL of CHRIST, for it is

the POWER of GOD unto SALVAT-

I ON to everyone that believeth.

19 Because that which may be known of

God is MANIFEST in THEM...

20 For the INVISIBLE THINGS of HIM

From the CREATION of the WORLD are

clearly seen, being UNDERSTOOD by the

THINGS, that are made even his

ETERNAL POWER and GODHEAD

So that they are WITHOUT

EXCUSE.

HEAVENLY EVENTS

HEAVENLY EVENTS NOT SEEN UPON the EARTH

Rev. 7:2 The FOUR SEALS OPENED and REALESED upon the EERTH are STOPED until GOD has

SEALED his 144,000 in their FOREHEAD.

Isaiah 40:22 IT IS HE THAT SIT

UPON the CIRCLE of the EARTH.

Dan. 12:9 And he said go thy way

Daniel for the WORDS are CLOSED up SEALED

Till the TIME of the END and NONE of the WICKED

SHALL UNDERSTAND, but the WISE SHALL

UNDERSTAND.

EARTH

Today Four of the SEVEN SEALS are NOW OPENED

Mat. 27:52,53 THE FIRST RESURRECTION HAS OCCURRED, THE OPENING of the FIFTH SEAL, which is the

COMING of the LORD and the 144,000, I Thess. 4:13. even so them which sleep in Jesus will God bring with him.

The TIME of the GREAT TRIBULATION the WRATH of GOD

THE TIME of the OPENING of the SIXTH SEAL

"Mat 24:21 For then shall be GREAT TRIBULATIONS,

such as was not since the beginning of the world to

this time, no, nor ever shall be."

Joel 2:3 A FIRE DEVOURETH BEFORE THEM, and

Behind them a FLAME BURN; the LAND is as the

GARDEN of EDEN before them..."

The SECOND COMING of CHRIST

EZEKIEL'S CHERUBIM

The FOUR ANGLES the FOUR SEALS

Jer. 9:10...both the fowl of the heaven

& the beast are fled they are gone".

The sealing of

144,000

SEAL of GOD

"Joel 1:16 Is not the meat cut off

Before our eyes, yea, joy & glad-

Ness from the house of our God.

Joel 1:17 The seeds is ROTTEN under their CLODS the GARDENS are laid desolate".

Joel 1:17. ..the barns are BROKEN DOWN for the corn is WITHERED.

Mat. 24:29 Immediately after the tribulation of those days shall the sun be

darkened, & the moon shall not give her light, & the stars shall fall from heaven,

& the powers of the heaven shall be shaken.

Zech. 14:1 Behold, the day of the Lord cometh, & thy spoil shall be divided in the

midst of thee. 2. For I will gather all nations against Jerusalem to battle; & the

city shall be taken, & the houses rifled, & the women ravished; & half of the city

Shall go into captivity.

Dan. 12:1 And there shall be a TIME of TROUBLE such as never was since there

Was a NATION ever to that same time.

" Rev. 6:12 And the sun become black as SACKCLOTH of hair, & the moon become

As BLOOD.....".

Joel 1:19 Then I said I, I will not feed you: that that die, let it die; and that that is to be cut off, let it be cut off; & let the rest eat every one the FLEASH of ANOTHER".

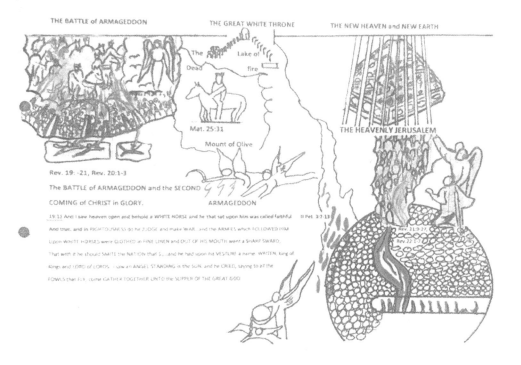

THE BATTLE of ARMAGEDDON THE GREAT WHITE THRONE THE NEW HEAVEN and NEW EARTH

The Lake of

Dead fire

Mat. 25:31

Mount of Olive

THE HEAVENLY JERUSALEM

Rev. 19: -21, Rev. 20:1-3

The BATTLE of ARMAGEDDON and the SECOND

COMING of CHRIST in GLORY. ARMAGEDDON

19:11 And I saw heaven open and behold a WHITE HORSE and he that sat upon him was called faithful   II Pet. 3:7-13

And true, and in RIGHTEOUSNESS do he JUDGE and make WAR, and the ARMIES which FOLLOWED HIM

Upon WHITE HORSES were CLOTHED in FINE LINEN and OUT OF HIS MOUTH went a SHARP SWARD,

That with it he should SMITE the NATION that S...and he had upon his VESTURE a name, WRITEN, King of

Kings and LORD of LORDS. I saw an ANGEL STANDING in the SUN, and he CRIED, saying to all the

FOWLS that FLY, come GATHER TOGETHER UNTO the SUPPER OF THE GREAT GOD

Climate Change Impacts

A collage of typical climate and weather- related events: heatwaves, droughts, hurricanes, wildfires, and loss of glacial ice. (Image credit:NOAA)
National Oceanic and Atmospheric Administration.

Not just with this Article, but all the Articles set before you in our Current Events, which occurred in 2023, those issues are caused by Climate Change. Such as Loss of Glacier Ice, Heatwaves brought on by Climate Change. July 2023 is the HOTTEST month ever recorded, climate change is Melting Mount Ranier's Glacier.

The IPCC's Sixty Assessment report, published in 2021 found that human emissions of heat-trapping gases have already warmed the climate by nearly 2 degrees Fahrenheit (1.1 degrees Celsius) since 1850-1900. Human activity is the cause of increased Greenhouse Gas Concentrations. Over the last century, burning of fossil fuels like coal and oil has increased the concentration of atmospheric carbon dioxide (CO_2). GLOBAL WARMING is the long term warming of the planets over all temperature, though this warming trend has been going on for a long time, Its pace has SIGNIFICANTLY INCREASED in the last HUNDRED YEARS due to the burning of fossil fuels. As the human population has increased so has the volume of fossil fuels burned. Dec 14, 2022.

What we are showing is King Alfred, the Great, who rose to world power when the great horn was broken.

The information above gives details on the time of the one-world government.

Current Devastations

A. Effects of Global Warming

This is a problem that occurred because of climate change.

1. Flooding
2. Wildfires
3. Effects of climate change

B. Climate Change Impacts

The impact of climate change, starting in 2023, is clearly seen, which is why we are bringing these issues before you. We have sixty million people believing and following the lie from Donald Trump, which is that "climate change is something the Democrats are saying is happening to hinder progress."

The ecosystem and communities in the United States and around the world are being impacted today by a collage of typical climate and weather-related events, such as floods, heatwaves, droughts, hurricanes, wildfires, and the loss of glacial ice.

It also includes sea level rise, changes in weather patterns like drought and flooding, and much more. Things that we depend upon and value—water, energy, transportation, wildlife, agriculture, ecosystems, and human health—are experiencing the effects of a changing climate.

A. Flooding Affects Millions in Bangladesh, India and Naples

There have been thousands of families forced to leave their homes to escape the floods that have claimed lives, destroyed crops, and ruined food stocks. Another issue to be considered is "widespread diseases."

B. **Deadly Floods Strike Greece and Turkey after Storms and Wildfires**

Deadly floods strike Greece and Turkey as extreme weather follows wildfires. With more than two feet of rain falling in less than two days, parts of Greece and Turkey that were still recovering from devastating wildfires have now been struck by flash flooding.

C. **Outage Grows in China after Areas Flooded to Save Beijing**

Anger builds in China after the government deliberately floods the town to save Beijing.

CURRENT EVENTS

Four million children in Pakistan have no safe water, a year after deadly floods

THAT STATEMENT TELLS US NOT ENOUGH IS BEING DONE TO IMPROVE DAMAGES

AFTER THE EFFECT OF CLIMATE CHANGE. WE'RE TALKING ABOUT CHILDRENS SUFFERING

While China is building a new cold burning power plant every week, adding further damage to the world

One year after catastrophic floods devastated swathes of Pakistan, some 4 million children in the South Asian nation remain without access to safe water, the United Nations Children's agency has warned.

In a news release Friday, UNICEF said it estimates that there are 8 million people in the country, around half of whom are children, who continue to live in flood- affected areas without clean water.

Millions of people across Bangladesh, India and Nepal have been affected by floods caused by monsoon rains. In Nepal, thousands of families have been forced to flee their homes to escape the floods that have claimed lives, destroyed homes and ruined food stocks. UNICEF is working with the government and partners to get help to those most in need.

SAPTARI, Nepal, 21 August 2017 – As the floodwaters receded, Asha Devi Raya, 30, came down from the roof of her house. She had spent the night up there along with her 28-day-old baby daughter, four other children, and her in-laws.

Relentless rainfall across much of Nepal has resulted in monsoon flooding and landslides. Twenty-seven of the country's 75 districts have been affected by the floods, affecting 160,293 families and displacing 51,244 families throughout the country. So far 123 lives have been lost, including 20 children.

For three days, Asha's family survived on handfuls of *murai* (puffed rice). Worryingly, Asha's baby was showing signs of weakness and rashes had appeared on her face.

"You have to make sure none of this filth gets to the baby," says Sunita Sulpe, Water, Sanitation and Hygiene Officer for UNICEF, referring to the sludge left behind by the flood, as she hands a hygiene kit to Asha.

The kit was one of more than 600 that UNICEF distributed in the district as part of its immediate response. Each kit contains two towels, soaps for washing and bathing, a comb, nail clipper, sanitary pads, sets of toothbrushes and a toothpaste, and a five metre rope that can be used as a clothesline.

Morocco Earth Quake Updates More Than 2,100 Dead In Rare, Powful Quake

The quake struck Morocco's High Atlas mountain range near Marrakech. The U.S. Geological Survey recorded the quake had 6.8 magnitude, The U.S. agency reported a 4.9-magnitude aftershock hit 19 minutes later. Death toll rises to 2,122, thousands more injured. In the village of Amizmiz, some areas have been entirely wiped out.
  In Marrakech and five provinces near the epicenter, officals said. At least 2,059 people injured -- including 1,404 critically.

MUCH INFORMATION HAS BEEN SET BEFORE US

Tenerife Wildfires Force Over 12,000 Evacuations

Wildfire on Spain's popular tourist island of Tenerife was started deliberately, official says according to the European Forest Fire information System, Spain heads the list of EU countries affected by wildfires so far this year, with 75,000 hectares (185,000 acres)burned ahead of Italy and Greece.
The fire currently an area of roughly 8,400 hectares (around 20,757 acres). according to local authorities. Flares are seen on the horizon as the fire advances though the forest toward the town of la Laguna Los Rodeos airport.

The Time of the Sun Clothed Woman

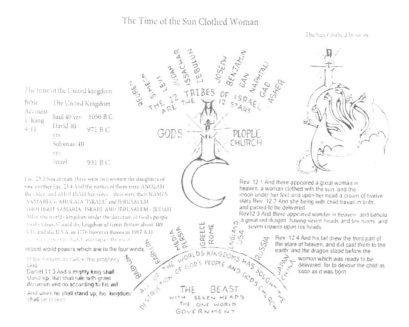

The Sun Clothed Woman

The time of the United kingdom

Bible Account
1. King 9:11

	The United Kingdom	
	Saul 40 yrs	1050 B.C.
	David 40 yrs	971 B.C.
	Solomon 40 yrs	
	Israel	931 B.C.

Eze. 23:2 Son of man, there were two women the daughters of one mother. Eze. 23:4 And the names of them were ANOLAH the elder, and AHOLIBAH her sister: thus were their NAMES SAMARIA is AHOLAH "ISRAEL" and JERUSALEM AHOLIBAH SAMARIA - ISRAEL AND JERUSALEM - JUDAH. All of the world's kingdom under the direction of God's people "God's Church" until the Kingdom of Great Britain about 149 A.D. and the U.S.A. in 1776 however Russia in 1917 A.D. ... ... the church and Japan the most

recent world powers which are to the four winds

of the heaven as said in the prophecy of God.
Daniel 11:3 And a mighty king shall stand up, that shall rule with great dominion and do according to his will.
And when he shall stand up, his kingdom shall be broken.

GOD'S PEOPLE CHURCH

THE 12 TRIBES OF ISRAEL ARE THE 12 STARS

REUBEN SIMEON THE LEVI JUDAH ISSACHAR ZEBULUN JOSEPH BENJAMIN DAN NAPHTALI GAD ASHER

Rev. 12:1 And there appeared a great woman in heaven, a woman clothed with the sun, and the moon under her feet and upon her head a crown of twelve stars. Rev. 12:2 And she being with child travail in birth, and pained to be delivered.
Rev. 12:3 And there appeared wonder in heaven, and behold a great red dragon, having seven heads and ten horns, and seven crowns upon his heads.

Rev. 12:4 And his tail drew the third part of the stars of heaven, and did cast them to the earth: and the dragon stood before the woman which was ready to be delivered, for to devour the child as soon as it was born.

BABYLON MEDIA PERSIA GREECE ROME ENGLAND U.S.A RUSSIA JAPAN CHINA

ALL OF THE WORLD'S KINGDOMS HAS SOUGHT THE DESTRUCTION OF GOD'S PEOPLE AND GOD'S CHURCH

THE BEAST WITH SEVEN HEADS THE ONE WORLD GOVERNMENT

Because this book is Prophecy, with recognition of issues pertaining to Existence of Life.

ABOUT THE AUTHOR

 As I think back, the first person I recall seeing was my grandmother; also, I had a brother. The one thing I remember is on Sundays, my grandmother tells me, "Little boy, get dressed, you're going to church."

And that was what my brother and I did. She could not sign her name; she would put an X on the line, but she had friends in church that kept an eye on us and would come and visit Grandmother.

I was playing with a friend of mine in the yard. He asked me if I knew how to curse. I didn't know what he meant, so I said no. He said, "I will show you how to curse." He started saying a lot of words that I didn't know what they meant. I just know what he was saying were bad things about my God, which I did not like. I made up my mind; I did not want him anymore for my friend.

He came over and asked Grandmother where I was. I had told grandmother I did not want him for my friend anymore; she asked why, and I explained he wanted to teach me to curse, but I didn't like cursing.

She told me she loved me for that, but I needed to talk to him and tell him; so next time he came over, that was what I did.

As I got older, I started smoking cigarettes and drinking beer. I thought it looked cool to stand around with a cigarette in my mouth. I would not smoke until I was around teens like myself.

Then when I was around eighteen years old, I married a girl and started having children. I keep a job and have taken care of my family. I have always been a person who loves reading the Bible.

So that has been my life—working, taking care of my family, going to church, and reading my Bible; that might seem like a dull life to some, but I am very pleased with it.

Printed in the USA
CPSIA information can be obtained
at www.ICGtesting.com
LVHW012248021024
792708LV00021B/575